The Complete
30-Day Whole Food
Cookbook for Beginners

The Simple & On-Budget Recipes will Help
You Start Adjusting Your Eating Habits

Aimee Tavares

© Copyright 2023 - All Rights Reserved

The content contained within this book may not be reproduced, duplicated or transmitted without direct written permission from the author or the publisher.

Under no circumstances will any blame or legal responsibility be held against the publisher, or author, for any damages, reparation, or monetary loss due to the information contained within this book, either directly or indirectly.

Legal Notice:

This book is copyright protected. It is only for personal use. You cannot amend, distribute, sell, use, quote or paraphrase any part, or the content within this book, without the consent of the author or publisher.

Disclaimer Notice:

Please note the information contained within this document is for educational and entertainment purposes only. All effort has been executed to present accurate, up to date, reliable, complete information. No warranties of any kind are declared or implied. Readers acknowledge that the author is not engaged in the rendering of legal, financial, medical or professional advice. The content within this book has been derived from various sources. Please consult a licensed professional before attempting any techniques outlined in this book.

By reading this document, the reader agrees that under no circumstances is the author responsible for any losses, direct or indirect, that are incurred as a result of the use of the information contained within this document, including, but not limited to, errors, omissions, or inaccuracies.

CONTENT

1   Introduction

2   Fundamentals of 30-Day Whole Foods

12   4-Week Meal Plan

14   Chapter 1 Breakfast Recipes

26   Chapter 2 Vegetable and Sides Recipes

38   Chapter 3 Poultry Recipes

50   Chapter 4 Beef, Pork, and Lamb Recipes

61   Chapter 5 Fish and Seafood Recipes

73   Chapter 6 Snack and Appetizer Recipes

87   Chapter 7 Dessert Recipes

99   Conclusion

100 Appendix 1 Measurement Conversion Chart

101 Appendix 2 Recipes Index

Introduction

If you're looking to start eating healthier, one of the best places to start is by incorporating more whole foods into your diet. And what better way to do that than with a cookbook specifically devoted to whole foods recipes? The 30-Day Whole Foods Cookbook is a great resource for anyone wanting to transition to a healthier way of eating. The book is divided into four weeks, with each week featuring recipes that focus on a different type of whole food. Week one focuses on fruits and vegetables, week two features whole grains, week three spotlights protein-rich foods, and week four highlights healthy fats. In addition to recipes, the book also includes tips on how to shop for and prepare whole foods and information on the health benefits of each type of food. Whether you're a complete novice in the kitchen or a seasoned pro, the 30-Day Whole Foods Cookbook has something for everyone. Make sure you have plenty of whole foods on hand so you don't get tempted to cheat. Batch cooking will help you save time and stay on track. This challenge is all about eating whole foods for 30 days. That means eating foods that are unprocessed and unrefined. This includes fruits, vegetables, whole grains, nuts, and seeds. The challenge may seem daunting at first, but it's not as difficult as it sounds. Start by slowly incorporating more whole foods into your diet. And be sure to plan so you have healthy meals and snacks on hand. With a little effort, you can easily stick to the challenge and reap the benefits of eating whole foods.

Fundamentals of 30-Day Whole Foods

What Is 30-Day Whole Foods?

Are you looking to jumpstart your healthy eating habits? Why not try a 30-Day Whole Foods challenge? Eating whole foods is a great way to improve your health and energy levels. It can also help you lose weight and feel better overall. If you want to improve your diet and eat more whole foods, you may consider a 30-Day Whole Foods challenge. This type of challenge requires you to eat only whole foods for 30 days and typically eliminates processed foods, added sugars, and refined grains from your diet. Whole foods are generally considered to be healthier than processed foods, as they're minimally processed and often contain more vitamins, minerals, and fiber. Eating a diet rich in whole foods has been linked with various health benefits, including a lower risk of chronic diseases such as heart disease, diabetes, and cancer. If you're thinking of undertaking a 30-Day Whole Foods challenge, it's important to plan and make sure you have enough whole foods on hand. You'll also want to make sure you're getting enough variety in your diet, as eating the same foods every day can quickly become monotonous. If you're looking to improve your eating habits and cut out processed foods, you may be considering a 30-Day Whole Foods challenge. The 30-Day Whole Foods is a month-long program that asks participants to eat only whole, unprocessed foods. This means no processed meats, grains, dairy,

legumes, alcohol, or added sugars. The challenge is meant to help you reset eating habits and break any reliance on unhealthy, processed foods. If you're thinking of embarking on a 30-Day Whole Foods challenge, there are a few things you should know. First, the challenge is not for the faint of heart. It's a major change from the Standard American Diet, and it can be tough to stick to at first. However, many people find that the challenge is well worth it, as it can lead to improved energy levels, better sleep, and increased focus. To succeed on the 30-Day Whole Foods, you'll need to be prepared. This means stocking your kitchen with whole, unprocessed foods.

30-Day Whole Food Challenges

The challenge is simple: for 30 days, eat whole foods. That means unprocessed, unrefined, and straight from nature. No artificial flavors, colors, or preservatives. The goal is to improve your overall health, energy levels, and quality of sleep. The first step is to assess your current diet. Track everything you eat and drink for 3 days, including water. Be as specific as possible, including portion sizes. This will give you a baseline to measure your progress. Then, it's time to clean out your pantry and fridge. Toss anything that doesn't fit the challenge criteria. This may seem drastic, but starting with a clean slate is important. Are you up for a challenge? If you're interested in eating healthier, then you may want to try the 30-Day Whole Foods challenge. This means eating ONLY whole foods for 30 days - no processed foods, no artificial ingredients, and no junk food. It may sound daunting, but it can be done! Here are a few tips to help you succeed. Plan ahead. This is key to any successful challenge. Decide what meals you're going to eat and make a grocery list accordingly. Prep meals in advance. This will help you stay on track when you're feeling hungry and don't have time to cook. Find a friend or family member to do the challenge with you. Having someone to support you will make it much easier. Allow yourself some flexibility. If you slip up and eat something that isn't allowed, don't beat yourself up. Just get back on track the next day. If you're considering taking on the

30-Day Whole Foods Challenge, congratulations! Eating whole foods is a great way to improve your health and vitality.

Planning is key. Take some time to map out your meals for the month. This will help you stay on track and avoid feeling overwhelmed. Get creative in the kitchen. There are plenty of delicious whole foods recipes out there. Experiment and find some new favorites. Don't be too hard on yourself. If you have a slip-up, don't beat yourself up. Just get back on track and keep going. Stay positive. Remember, this is a challenge to improve your health. Approach it with excitement and determination, and you'll be successful. Reach out for support. If you need some motivation or encouragement, there are plenty of people who have taken on the challenge before. One potential challenge for the 30-Day Whole Foods Challenge is giving up processed foods. Processed foods are foods that have been altered from their natural state, usually for the purpose of extending their shelf life or making them more convenient to eat. This typically means that processed foods are high in unhealthy additives like salt, sugar, and fat, and low in important nutrients like fiber and vitamins. Another potential challenge is making the switch to whole, unprocessed foods can be costly, as these foods are often more expensive than their processed counterparts. Finally, it can be difficult to find the time to cook healthy meals from scratch, especially if you are used to eating convenience foods. However, the rewards of eating a healthy, whole-food diet are well worth the effort, and with a little planning and preparation, the 30-Day Whole Foods Challenge can be a success!

How to Follow 30-Day Whole Foods Challenges?

If you're looking to improve your diet and reset your eating habits, a 30-Day whole-foods challenge can be a great way to do it. While there are many different ways to approach a 30-Day Whole Foods challenge. When it comes to food, we all have different preferences. Some of us like our food to be cooked a certain way, while others prefer it raw. The 30-Day Whole Foods challenge is a great way to jumpstart a healthy lifestyle. By eating whole foods, you will be getting the most nutrients possible and satisfying your hunger. Some of us like to eat clean, whole foods, while others don't mind a few processed items here and there. And some of us like to challenge ourselves to eat clean for 30 days, while others find the thought of that daunting. If you're someone who likes a challenge, and you're interested in eating clean for 30 days, here are five steps to follow to make sure you're successful:

1. Define Your Goals: Choose a start date and commit to the challenge. Before you start your challenge, take some time to think about what you want to achieve. Are you looking to eat more nutrient-rich foods? Cut out processed foods? Reset your sugar cravings? Before you start your challenge, it's important to set a goal. Why do you want to eat clean for 30 days? What do you hope to accomplish? Having a clear goal in mind will help you stay motivated throughout the challenge. Once you know what your goals are, you can tailor your challenge to help you reach them.

2. Make a Plan: Make a plan for each day, including meals and snacks. One of the keys to success with any challenge is planning. This is especially true with a 30-Day whole foods challenge, where you'll need to be extra mindful of what you're eating. Spend some time each week on meal planning and prepping so that you have healthy options on hand when you get hungry. Map out what you're going to eat each day. This doesn't have to be complicated – a simple list of meals and snacks will do. But having a plan will help you stay on track and avoid unhealthy temptations.

3. Be Realistic: Be realistic and Stay motivated by keeping a food journal and tracking your progress. Making the switch to a whole foods diet can be daunting, but it's important to be realistic about what you can accomplish in 30 days. Here are a few tips to help you make the transition: Start slowly and build up. If you're used to eating processed foods, your body may not be able to handle a sudden switch to a 30-Day Whole Foods diet. Start by slowly adding more whole foods to your diet and cutting back on processed foods. Don't try to do too much at once. Making big changes to your diet can be overwhelming. Take it one step at a time and focus on incorporating more whole foods into your meals and snacks. Be prepared. Have healthy snacks and meals on hand so you're not tempted to reach for unhealthy options. Planning will help you stay on track and make it more likely that you'll stick with the challenge. Be flexible. There will be days when you Slip up or don't have

4. Shop Smart: Fill your pantry and fridge with healthy, whole foods. This way, you won't be tempted to eat junk food. Stock your kitchen with whole foods. The 30-Day Whole Foods Challenge is a great way to save money on groceries and eat healthier. By following the challenge, you'll learn how to cook simple, healthy meals using whole foods. You'll also save money by avoiding processed foods, which are often more expensive. Plan your meals. This will help you save money by avoiding impulse purchases. Stick to a budget. Decide how much you're willing to spend on groceries each week, and then stick to it. Shop at a variety of stores. Compare prices between different stores to find the best deal.

5. Reward Yourself: Stay motivated by keeping a food journal and tracking your progress. Reward yourself for completing the challenge! If you've completed a 30-Day whole foods challenge, congratulations! You've committed to eating healthy and nourishing your body. Now it's time to reward yourself for all your hard work. One way to reward yourself is to treat yourself to a healthy meal or snack. You can cook yourself a nutritious meal using all the whole foods, or you can go out to eat at a restaurant that specializes in healthy fare. Another way to treat yourself is to buy yourself a new piece of workout equipment or clothing, or to sign up for a fitness class. You can also simply take some time for yourself to relax and rejuvenate. Get a massage, take a yoga class, or take a long bath. Whatever you do, make sure it's something that makes you feel good and that you enjoy. You deserve it!

Why Are the 30-Day Whole Foods Challenges Difficult?

30-Day Whole foods challenges are difficult for a variety of reasons. For one, they require a complete overhaul of your diet, which can be tough to stick to. Additionally, they can be pricey, as buying whole, unprocessed foods can be more expensive than conventional foods. Finally, they can be time-consuming, as cooking whole foods from scratch can take longer than heating something from the freezer. However, the benefits of a 30-Day Whole Foods challenge—such as improved health, weight loss, and increased energy—are worth the effort! 30-Day Whole foods challenges can be difficult for several reasons. Here are some other reasons why a 30-Day Whole Foods challenge may be difficult for you:

- ▲ You're used to eating processed and junk food.
- ▲ You're used to eating out a lot.
- ▲ You have a busy lifestyle and don't have time to cook.
- ▲ You're not used to cooking at home.
- ▲ You don't know how to cook healthy meals.
- ▲ You're used to eating high-calorie meals.
- ▲ You're used to eating large portions.
- ▲ You're used to snacking often.
- ▲ You have a sweet tooth.
- ▲ You love salty foods.
- ▲ You're a picky eater.
- ▲ You have food allergies or intolerances.
- ▲ You have a tight budget.
- ▲ You live in a food desert.
- ▲ You don't have access to healthy food.

Advantages of 30-Day Whole Foods

If you're considering 30-Day Whole Foods, or have already started one, you may be wondering what the benefits are. After all, it's a pretty big commitment to give up all grains, dairy, soy, legumes, alcohol, and added sugars for 30 days. So what do you get in return? If you're looking to improve your health and reset your diet, a whole-foods reset may be just what you need. Here are some advantages of resetting your diet with whole foods:

Improved Digestion: For many people, giving up grains, dairy, and legumes can lead to improved digestion. These food groups can be difficult to digest for some people, and eliminating them can lead to less bloating, less gas, and fewer digestive issues.

More Energy: When you're not constantly dealing with digestive issues, you may find that you have more energy. This is because your body can better absorb nutrients from the food you're eating.

Clearer Skin: For some people, eliminating dairy and sugar can lead to clearer skin.

Here are some other potential benefits of 30-Day Whole Foods

▲ You'll consume fewer toxins.
▲ You'll eat more nutrient-rich foods.
▲ You'll likely lose weight.
▲ You'll have more energy.
▲ You'll sleep better.
▲ You'll reduce inflammation.
▲ You'll detox your body.
▲ You'll improve your digestion.
▲ You'll boost your immune system.
▲ You'll lower your risk for chronic diseases.
▲ You'll feel happier and less stressed.
▲ You'll have clearer skin.
▲ You'll have stronger hair

What Foods Are Allowed to be Eaten?

When it comes to food, there are few restrictions on what you can bring on a plane. However, the TSA does have guidelines about what types of food are allowed through security. Here are some general tips to keep in mind when packing food for your next flight:

▲ All liquids, gels, and aerosols must be in containers that are 3.4 ounces (100 milliliters) or less and placed in a single, clear, quart-sized bag.

▲ Solid food items are generally allowed through security.

▲ If you are bringing a baby or toddler with you on your flight, you are allowed to bring baby food and formula through security.

▲ If you are traveling with special dietary needs, you are allowed to bring food items that are necessary for your health and well-being.

So, what types of food are allowed on a plane? Anything that is not a liquid or gel is allowed. There are a variety of food items that are allowed to be

eaten. However, not all foods are allowed to be eaten in every country. For example, in some countries, pork is not allowed to be eaten. In others, beef is not allowed. It is important to check with the local authorities to find out what specific food items are allowed to be eaten in the country that you are visiting.

What Foods Are Not Allowed to be Eaten?

There are a few different types of food that are not allowed to be eaten. The first type is poisonous food. This includes things like poisonous mushrooms, fish that have been poisonous, and so on. The second type is food that is contaminated. This includes food that has been tainted with bacteria or other contaminants. The third type is food that is unhealthy. This includes food that is high in saturated fat, sugar, or salt.

Poisonous: There are many reasons why poisonous food is not allowed to be eaten. For one, they can be incredibly dangerous to our health. Poisonous food can contain harmful toxins that can cause serious illness or even death. Additionally, poisonous food can be difficult to digest and can cause digestive problems. Finally, poisonous food can also be environmentally harmful, as it can contaminate water supplies and soil.

Contaminated: There are many reasons why contaminated food is not allowed to be eaten. The main reason is that it can make you sick. Contaminated food can contain bacteria, viruses, or toxins that can cause food poisoning, diarrhea, or other serious illnesses. Another reason why contaminated food is not allowed to be eaten is that it can spread diseases. If you eat contaminated food, you can spread the bacteria or viruses to other

people. This can cause a foodborne illness outbreak. Contaminated food can also contain harmful chemicals. These chemicals can be toxic and can cause serious health problems. So, it is important to avoid eating contaminated food. If you think you have eaten contaminated food, you should see a doctor right away.

Unhealthy: Unhealthy food is not allowed to be eaten because it can lead to several health problems. These include obesity, heart disease, high blood pressure, and type 2 diabetes. Unhealthy food is also high in calories and low in nutrients, which can contribute to weight gain and other health problems. If you are taking Coumadin (warfarin), it is important to be aware of foods that can interact with the medication and affect its effectiveness. Here are some foods that you should avoid while taking Coumadin:

Green leafy vegetables: These vegetables contain high levels of vitamin K, which can interact with Coumadin and reduce its effectiveness. Examples of green leafy vegetables to avoid include spinach, kale, and collard greens.

Cauliflower: Like green leafy vegetables, cauliflower also contains high levels of vitamin K.

Soybean products: Soybeans and soybean products (tofu, soy milk, etc.) contain a substance known as genistein, which can interact with Coumadin and reduce its effectiveness.

Alcohol: Alcohol can interact with Coumadin and increase the risk of bleeding.

Grapefruit: Grapefruit contains a substance that can interact with Coumadin. So, it is good for health to avoid grapefruit while taking Coumadin.

Suggestions and Cautions

If you're considering doing a 30-Day Whole Foods challenge, congratulations! This is a great way to reset your body and give your digestive system a break. Here are a few suggestions to help you make the most of your challenge:

Plan ahead: This challenge is not something you want to try to wing. Decide which 30 days you're going to do the challenge and make a grocery list accordingly. The 30-Day Whole Foods Challenge is a great way to jumpstart your healthy eating habits. By planning and being prepared, you can make the most of the challenge and see amazing results. Meal planning is key to success on any diet, but especially on a 30-Day Whole Foods Challenge. Stock your pantry and fridge with healthy, whole foods ingredients so you always have something to eat. Here are a few tips to help you plan and make the most of the challenge:

▲ Decide what your goals are. What do you hope to accomplish by taking on the challenge? Whether it's weight loss, more energy, or simply eating healthier, having a clear goal in mind will help you stay on track.

▲ Make a list of all the foods you'll need. This includes everything from staples like fruits, vegetables, and whole grains to more specific items like almond milk and quinoa.

▲ Stock your pantry and fridge. Before the challenge begins, make sure you have all the foods you need on hand. This will make it easier to stick to the challenge and avoid any temptation to cheat.

Stick to whole, unprocessed foods. This means no pre-packaged meals or snacks, no processed meats or cheeses, and no artificial sweeteners. If you're like me, you love a good challenge. That's why I've decided to do the 30-Day Whole Foods Challenge. For 30 days, I'm going to eat nothing but whole foods. That means no processed foods, no artificial ingredients, and no added sugar. I know this is going to be a challenge, but I'm up for it. I want to see how my body feels when I'm eating nothing but whole foods. I'm also curious to see if I have more energy and feel better overall.

Cook at home as much as possible. Eating out can be tricky on 30-Day Whole Foods, so it's best to cook at home as much as you can. One of the best things about cooking at home is that you know exactly what's going into your food. No more wondering about hidden ingredients or added sugars - when you cook at home, you have complete control over your ingredients. Another great thing about cooking at home is that it can save you money. Eating out all the time can get expensive, but cooking at home is a great way to save some cash.

Get creative with your meals. Just because you're avoiding processed foods doesn't mean you have to eat boring meals. Get creative with your recipes and experiment with new ingredients. This can be a great way to jumpstart your healthy eating habits and see some real results. To get started, simply commit to eating only whole foods for 30 days. This means no processed or refined foods, no fast food, and no sugary drinks. Fill your diet with fresh fruits and vegetables, whole grains, lean proteins, and healthy fats. To make sure you stick to your goals, plan your meals and stock your kitchen with healthy ingredients. Meal prep can help you stay on track, and it's also a great way to save time and money. Throughout the challenge, pay attention to how you're feeling. Do you have more energy? Are you sleeping better? Are your skin and hair looking healthier? Be sure to celebrate your successes, no matter how big or small.

Here are a few things to keep in mind as you embark on this challenge:

▲ Don't be too hard on yourself. This challenge is about making small, sustainable changes. If you slip up, don't beat yourself up. Just get back on track and keep going.

▲ Be prepared for cravings. When you first cut out processed foods, you may find yourself craving them more than usual. This is normal! Stick to your plan and the cravings will eventually subside.

▲ Drink plenty of water. Water is essential for good health.

▲ Don't go into this challenge expecting to lose a ton of weight. While you may lose some weight, the goal of this challenge is to eat healthier, not necessarily to lose weight.

▲ You may be surprised at how difficult it is to give up some of your favorite unhealthy foods. Be prepared for some temptations and cravings.

▲ Eating out can be tricky on this challenge. It's best to cook at home as much as possible.

▲ You may need to get creative with your meals. Eating the same thing every day can get boring.

▲ You may not have as much energy at first.

4-Week Meal Plan

Week 1

Day 1:
Breakfast: Baby Kale Salad with Bacon Egg
Lunch: Healthy Cabbage Slaw
Snack: Roasted Potatoes
Dinner: Chicken Tagine with Pomegranates Seeds
Dessert: Nuts and Berries Jelly

Day 2:
Breakfast: Crispy Bacon Omelets
Lunch: Onion Cucumber Salad
Snack: Antioxidant Nuts Mix
Dinner: Mexican-style Beef Stew
Dessert: Aromatic Lemony Apples

Day 3:
Breakfast: Cinnamon Waffle
Lunch: Zucchini Slaw
Snack: Pineapple Salad with Avocado
Dinner: Aromatic Cinnamon Pork Chops
Dessert: Chocolate Almond Banana Squares

Day 4:
Breakfast: Avocado with Scrambled Eggs
Lunch: Tomato Gazpacho
Snack: Sweet Potato Sticks
Dinner: Curried Chicken with Sweet Potatoes & Peas
Dessert: Berries Cream

Day 5:
Breakfast: Eggs and Brussels Sprouts
Lunch: Easy Grilled Asparagus
Snack: Spiced Turkey Wings
Dinner: Salmon Bake
Dessert: Tropical Coconut and Pear Delight

Day 6:
Breakfast: Delicious Tomatoes & Cashews Casserole
Lunch: Spiced Broccoli
Snack: Crispy Squash Fries
Dinner: Garlicky Roast Lamb Leg
Dessert: Almond and Coconut Apple Dessert

Day 7:
Breakfast: Cheese Bell Pepper and Olives Frittata
Lunch: Colorful Summer Vegetable Bake
Snack: Cajun French Fries
Dinner: Juicy Chicken with Blueberry Lime Salsa
Dessert: Easy Pear Wedges

Week 2

Day 1:
Breakfast: Egg and Beef Burgers
Lunch: Herbed Eggplant Slices
Snack: Nutty Carrots
Dinner: Tasty Tiger Prawns and Bitter Melon
Dessert: Currant Poached Peaches

Day 2:
Breakfast: Sausage and Mushroom Frittata
Lunch: Savory Beans with Bacon
Snack: Simple Paprika Potato Slices
Dinner: Crispy Pork Roast
Dessert: Delicious Apple and Peach Compote

Day 3:
Breakfast: Healthy Pumpkin Sandwich
Lunch: Zucchini with Scrambled Eggs
Snack: Savory Sweet Potatoes
Dinner: Grilled Chicken with Refreshing Cucumber Radish Salsa
Dessert: Cinnamon Strawberry Cream

Day 4:
Breakfast: Mushroom Sliders
Lunch: Tasty Tuna Stuffed Tomatoes
Snack: Garlicky Bell Pepper and Tomato
Dinner: Catfish and Veggie Gumbo
Dessert: Cashew Apple Stew

Day 5:
Breakfast: Chocolate Cereal
Lunch: Mashed Coconut Pumpkin
Snack: Carrots and Tomatoes Salad
Dinner: Pork Roast with Yucca
Dessert: Traditional Berry Pie

Day 6:
Breakfast: Coconut Pancake
Lunch: Baked Brussels Sprouts
Snack: "Hummus" of Spinach and Carrot
Dinner: Grilled herbed Chicken
Dessert: Figs & Pecans Stuffed Apples

Day 7:
Breakfast: Cheesy Bok Choi Quiche
Lunch: Yummy Broccoli and Hazelnuts
Snack: Marinated Spiced Eggs
Dinner: Salmon and Tomato Stew
Dessert: Dark Chocolate Cake

Week 3

Day 1:
Breakfast: Delicious Zucchini & Chicken Quiche
Lunch: Aromatic Dill Carrots
Snack: Tortilla Chips
Dinner: Juicy Pork Chops
Dessert: Lemon and berries Cream

Day 2:
Breakfast: Cheesy Cauliflower
Lunch: Simple Kale and Celery Dish
Snack: Herbed Button Mushrooms
Dinner: Spiced Chicken
Dessert: Stewed Figs and Pine Nuts

Day 3:
Breakfast: Eggs Benedict
Lunch: Spiced Tofu and Zucchini Skewers
Snack: Almond Crusted Zucchini Slices
Dinner: Delicious Garlic Shrimp
Dessert: Nutty Carrot Cake

Day 4:
Breakfast: Homemade Carrot & Pecan Muffins
Lunch: Vegetables Roast
Snack: Bacon Chicken Skewers
Dinner: Smoky Baby Back Ribs
Dessert: Silky Strawberry Marmalade

Day 5:
Breakfast: Vegetable Quiche
Lunch: Herbed Spaghetti Squash
Snack: Cheesy Tomatoes with Basil Dressing
Dinner: Thai Chicken and Veggie Stew
Dessert: Simple Raspberry Cream

Day 6:
Breakfast: Veggies and Egg Casserole
Lunch: Healthy Cabbage, Carrot & Apple Stew
Snack: Tasty Goat Skewers
Dinner: Spicy Cajun Roast Beef
Dessert: Energy Booster Bars

Day 7:
Breakfast: Crispy Bacon Omelets
Lunch: Tomato Pasta with Basil
Snack: Caprese Eggplant Roll Ups
Dinner: Cheese Chicken Meatballs
Dessert: Almond Pomegranate Fudge

Week 4

Day 1:
Breakfast: Baby Kale Salad with Bacon Egg
Lunch: Squash and Sweet Potato Soup
Snack: Pineapple Salad with Avocado
Dinner: Italian-Style Turkey Breasts
Dessert: Nuts and Berries Jelly

Day 2:
Breakfast: Avocado with Scrambled Eggs
Lunch: Onion Cucumber Salad
Snack: Sweet Potato Sticks
Dinner: Sea Bass with Juicy Broccoli
Dessert: Aromatic Lemony Apples

Day 3:
Breakfast: Cheese Bell Pepper and Olives Frittata
Lunch: Zucchini Slaw
Snack: Crispy Squash Fries
Dinner: Hot Barbequed Steak
Dessert: Chocolate Almond Banana Squares

Day 4:
Breakfast: Egg and Beef Burgers
Lunch: Easy Grilled Asparagus
Snack: Delicious Chili Hash Browns
Dinner: Delicious Caprese Chicken
Dessert: Berries Cream

Day 5:
Breakfast: Sausage and Mushroom Frittata
Lunch: Spiced Broccoli
Snack: Cajun French Fries
Dinner: Baked Garlicky Snapper
Dessert: Tropical Coconut and Pear Delight

Day 6:
Breakfast: Healthy Pumpkin Sandwich
Lunch: Colorful Summer Vegetable Bake
Snack: Nutty Carrots
Dinner: Spicy Barbecued Spareribs
Dessert: Almond and Coconut Apple Dessert

Day 7:
Breakfast: Avocado with Scrambled Eggs
Lunch: Herbed Eggplant Slices
Snack: Simple Paprika Potato Slices
Dinner: Turkey and Broccoli Balls
Dessert: Easy Pear Wedges

Chapter 1 Breakfast Recipes

15	Baby Kale Salad with Bacon Egg	20	Cheesy Cauliflower
15	Egg and Beef Burgers	20	Homemade Carrot & Pecan Muffins
16	Delicious Tomatoes & Cashews Casserole	21	Crispy Bacon Omelets
		21	Cinnamon Waffle
16	Cheese Bell Pepper and Olives Frittata	22	Avocado with Scrambled Eggs
17	Veggies and Egg Casserole	22	Eggs and Brussels Sprouts
17	Chocolate Cereal	23	Vegetable Quiche
18	Healthy Pumpkin Sandwich	23	Mushroom Sliders
18	Sausage and Mushroom Frittata	24	Delicious Zucchini & Chicken Quiche
19	Coconut Pancake	25	Eggs Benedict
19	Cheesy Bok Choi Quiche		

Baby Kale Salad with Bacon Egg

Prep time: 5 minutes | Cook time: 0 minutes | Serves: 2

1 teaspoon minced garlic

Pinch of salt

1 tablespoon extra-virgin olive oil

2 teaspoons red-wine vinegar

Pinch of ground pepper

3 cups lightly packed baby kale

1 piece cooked bacon, chopped

1 fried or poached large egg

1. Mash salt and garlic with a fork/side of chef's knife. 2. Mix pepper, vinegar, oil and garlic paste in a bowl then add kale; toss till coated. 3. Serve kale salad with egg and bacon over.

Per Serving: Calories 360; Fat 37g; Sodium 317mg; Carbs 7g; Fiber 3g; Sugar 1g; Protein 4g

Egg and Beef Burgers

Prep time: 5 minutes | Cook time: 25 minutes | Serves: 4

5 eggs

1 lb. ground beef meat

½ cup sausages; ground

8 slices bacon

3 sundried tomatoes; chopped

2 tablespoons. almond meal

2 teaspoons. basil leaves; chopped

1 teaspoon. garlic; finely minced

A drizzle of avocado oil

Black pepper to the taste

1. mix beef meat with 1 egg, almond meal, tomatoes, basil, pepper and garlic, stir well and form 4 burgers. 2. Heat up a pan over high heat, add burgers, cook for 5 minutes on each side, Place them to plates and leave aside. 3. Heat up the pan over -high heat, add sausages, stir; cook for 5 minutes and Place them to a plate. 4. Heat up the pan again, add bacon, cook for 4 minutes, drain excess grease. 5. Fry the 4 eggs in a pan with a drizzle of oil over -high heat and place them on top of burgers. Add sausage and bacon and serve.

Per Serving: Calories 90; Fat 6.5g; Sodium 186mg; Carbs 0.6g; Fiber 0g; Sugar 0.3g; Protein 5.8g

Delicious Tomatoes & Cashews Casserole

Prep time: 10 minutes | Cook time: 4 hours | Serves: 4

2 teaspoons onion powder

¾ cup cashews, soaked for 30 minutes, drained

1 teaspoon garlic powder

½ teaspoon sage, dried

Salt and black pepper to the taste

1 yellow onion, chopped

2 tablespoons parsley, chopped

3 garlic cloves, minced

1 tablespoon olive oil

5 tomatoes, cubed

½ teaspoon red pepper flakes

1. In blender, mix cashews with onion powder, garlic powder, sage, salt and pepper well. Add oil to slow cooker slow cooker and Place tomatoes, pepper flakes, garlic, onion, salt, pepper and parsley. 2. Add cashews sauce, toss, cover, cook on High for 4 hours, serve for breakfast.

Per Serving: Calories 323; Fat 34g; Sodium 314mg; Carbs 6g; Fiber 3g; Sugar 0g; Protein 5g

Cheese Bell Pepper and Olives Frittata

Prep time: 10 minutes | Cook time: 6 hours | Serves: 4

1-pound goat cheese, crumbled

2 tablespoons olive oil

1 yellow onion, chopped

¼ teaspoon turmeric powder

3 tablespoons garlic, minced

4 eggs, Mixed

3 red bell peppers, chopped

A pinch of salt and black pepper

½ cup kalamata olives, pitted and halved

1 teaspoon basil, dried

1 teaspoon oregano, dried

1 tablespoon lemon juice

1. Add the oil to slow cooker, spread cheese all over, add onion, turmeric, garlic, bell pepper, olives, basil, oregano, lemon juice, eggs, salt and pepper, toss a bit, cover and cook on Low temp setting for 6 hours. 2. serve for breakfast.

Per Serving: Calories 334; Fat 34g; Sodium 314mg; Carbs 6g; Fiber 3g; Sugar 1g; Protein 5g

Veggies and Egg Casserole

Prep time: 10 minutes | Cook time: 30 minutes | Serves: 4

8 eggs
½ cup almond milk
2 cups shredded sweet potatoes
1 cup shredded carrots
½ tablespoon olive oil
½ teaspoon dried parsley
¼ teaspoon pepper
¼ teaspoon paprika
¼ teaspoon garlic powder

1. Add the olive oil to the Instant Pot and set it to "SAUTE". When the oil becomes hot and sizzling, add the carrots and sweet potatoes. Add the herbs and spices, stir well and cook the veggies for about 23 minutes. 2. Meanwhile, beat the eggs and almond milk in a bowl. 3. Pour the mixture over the carrots and stir to incorporate well. Put the lid on and seal, hit "MANUAL". Set the cooking time to 7 minutes and cook on HIGH. 4. Press "KEEP WARM/CANCEL" after you hear the beep to turn the Instant Pot off. Move the pressure release handle from "Sealing" to "Venting" to do a quick pressure release and open the lid carefully. Serve and enjoy!

Per Serving: Calories 316; Fat 27.7g; Sodium 530mg; Carbs 2g; Fiber 0.3g; Sugar 1.6g; Protein 9.8g

Chocolate Cereal

Prep time: 5 minutes | Cook time: 0 minutes | Serves: 1

¼ cup slivered almonds
1 tablespoon chia seeds
2 tablespoon flaxseeds
1 tablespoon shredded coconut
A pinch of Stevia
2 tablespoon cocoa nibs
Unsweetened almond milk

1. Mix all the ingredients except the milk. Pour in the milk, stir and serve.

Per Serving: Calories 649; Fat 55.2g; Sodium 1336mg; Carbs 15.2g; Fiber 9.2g; Sugar 2.1g; Protein 21.3g

Healthy Pumpkin Sandwich

Prep time: 25 minutes | Cook time: 10 minutes | Serves: 2

1 oz. pumpkin flesh; peeled

4 slices paleo coconut bread

1 small avocado; pitted and peeled

1 carrot; finely grated

1 lettuce leaf; torn into 4 pieces

1. Put pumpkin in a tray, Put in the oven at 350°F and bake for 10 minutes. 2. Take pumpkin out of the oven, leave aside for 23 minutes. Place to a bowl and mash it a bit. Put avocado in bowl and also mash it with a fork. 3. Spread avocado on 2 bread slices, add grated carrot, mashed pumpkin and 2 lettuce pieces on each and top them with the rest of the bread slices.

Per Serving: Calories 620; Fat 49.6g; Sodium 1746mg; Carbs 4.7g; Fiber 1.2g; Sugar 1.7g; Protein 29.8g

Sausage and Mushroom Frittata

Prep time: 5 minutes | Cook time: 35 minutes | Serves: 4

10 eggs

2 tablespoons melted ghee

1 cup spinach; chopped

½ lb. sausage; chopped

1 cup mushrooms; chopped

1 small yellow onion; chopped

A pinch of sea salt

Black pepper to the taste

1. Heat up a pan with the ghee over high heat, add sausage pieces, stir and brown for a couple of minutes. 2. Add onion, mushroom, spinach, a pinch of salt and black pepper to the taste, stir and cook for a few more minutes. 3. Add Mix eggs, spread evenly and stir gently. 4. Put in the oven at 350°F and bake for 20 minutes.

Per Serving: Calories 201; Fat 14g; Sodium 1314mg; Carbs 3.1g; Fiber 0.6g; Sugar 1.6g; Protein 13.3g

Coconut Pancake

Prep time: 5 minutes | Cook time: 5 minutes | Serves: 2

1 fresh egg

½ cup coconut flour

1 cup coconut milk

1 teaspoon vanilla

½ teaspoon baking powder

¼ teaspoon salt

¼ teaspoon cinnamon

1 tablespoon olive oil

1. Place coconut flour, baking powder, vanilla, and cinnamon in a bowl. Stir and mix well. Pour coconut milk and egg into the mixture then mix well. Preheat a nonstick pan then brush with olive oil. 2. Pour two tablespoons of the mixture then cook for 2 minutes then flip them and cook for 2 minutes until both sides are brown.

Per Serving: Calories 71; Fat 4.3g; Sodium 62mg; Carbs 0.4g; Fiber 0g; Sugar 0.2g; Protein 6.3g

Cheesy Bok Choi Quiche

Prep time: 5 minutes | Cook time: 25 minutes | Serves: 4

¼ cup softened cream cheese

1 pastured egg

1 teaspoon minced garlic

¼ cup chopped Bok Choi

¾ cup almond flour

½ cup cheddar cubes

4 tablespoons yogurt

4 tablespoons fresh water

1. Preheat an oven to 350°F and grease a pan with cooking spray. Place the egg and softened cream cheese in a bowl then beat using a hand mixer until soft and fluffy. 2. Add in minced garlic, almond flour, chopped Bok Choi and cheddar cubes into the batter then mix using a wooden spatula. Pour yogurt and water into the mixture then stir thoroughly. 3. Place the mixture to the prepared pan then spread evenly. Bake for 25 minutes until set and lightly golden brown. 4. Once it is done, remove from the oven and serve warm.

Per Serving: Calories 107; Fat 7.7g; Sodium 387mg; Carbs 0.4g; Fiber 0g; Sugar 0g; Protein 7.8g

Cheesy Cauliflower

Prep time: 5 minutes | Cook time: 7 minutes | Serves: 4

1 cup cauliflower florets

2 tablespoons grated mozzarella cheese

2 tablespoons heavy cream

1. Preheat a steamer then cook the cauliflower florets for 2 minutes. Place the steamed cauliflowers in a microwave safe bowl then add heavy cream into it. Stir well. 2. Sprinkle mozzarella cheese over the cauliflower then microwave until the cheese is melted. 3. Serve warm.

Per Serving: Calories 249; Fat 15.5g; Sodium 367mg; Carbs 1.1g; Fiber 0.2g; Sugar 0g; Protein 20.5g

Homemade Carrot & Pecan Muffins

Prep time: 15 minutes | Cook time: 15 minutes | Serves: 8

¼ cup coconut oil

½ cup almond milk

½ cup chopped pecans

1 teaspoon apple pie spice

1 cup shredded carrots

3 eggs

⅓ cup pure & organic applesauce

1 cup ground almonds

1½ cups water

1. Pour the water into the instant pot and lower the trivet. Place the coconut oil, almond milk, eggs, applesauce, almonds and apple pie spice, in a bowl. 2. Beat the mixture well, until it becomes fluffy. Fold in the carrots and pecans. Pour the batter into 8 silicone muffin cups and place them on top of the trivet. Put the lid on and close it. 3. Press "MANUAL" button and set the cooking time to 15 minutes. When the timer goes off, hit "KEEP WARM/CANCEL" to turn the Instant Pot off. Move the pressure release handle from "Sealing" to "Venting" to do a quick pressure release. 4. Remove the muffins.

Per Serving: Calories 232; Fat 18.7g; Sodium 742mg; Carbs 1.4g; Fiber 0g; Sugar 1g; Protein 10.5g

Crispy Bacon Omelets

Prep time: 5 minutes | Cook time: 3 minutes | Serves: 1

2 Fresh eggs
½ cup chopped bacon
1 tablespoon olive oil
½ teaspoon pepper
¼ teaspoon salt

1. Crack the eggs in a bowl. 2. Spiced Spice with salt and pepper then Mix until mixed. 3. Add chopped bacon into the egg mixture then stir a little. 4. Preheat olive oil into the pan over moderate heat. 5. Pour the mixture into the pan then cook well. 6. Place to a serving dish then serve.

Per Serving: Calories 288; Fat 26g; Sodium 311mg; Carbs 10g; Fiber 2g; Sugar 7g; Protein 3g

Cinnamon Waffle

Prep time: 5 minutes | Cook time: 10 minutes | Serves: 2

¾ cup flaxseeds
1½ teaspoons baking powder
¼ teaspoon salt
3 fresh eggs
4 tablespoons water
2 tablespoons avocado oil
2 teaspoons cinnamon

1. Add and mix flaxseeds, baking powder, and salt in bowl. 2. Pour water into the dry mixture then adds eggs and avocado oil. Stir in cinnamon then mix until smooth. 3. Preheat a waffle maker then pour a scoop of the mixture into it. 4. Once it is done, remove from the waffle maker then place on a serving dish.

Per Serving: Calories 336; Fat 32g; Sodium 313mg; Carbs 11g; Fiber 3g; Sugar 4g; Protein 3g

Avocado with Scrambled Eggs

Prep time: 5 minutes | Cook time: 5 minutes | Serves: 3

1 tablespoon butter
5 pastured eggs
1 tablespoon water
¼ teaspoon black pepper
1 teaspoon chopped celery
½ cup avocado cubes

1. Add and mix all ingredients except butter in a bowl then stir well. 2. Preheat a skillet then place butter in it. 3. Once it is melted, pour the egg mixture into the skillet and cook. 4. Stirring for about 4 minutes until the egg is cooked well. 5. Place to a serving dish then enjoy.

Per Serving: Calories 336; Fat 34g; Sodium 314mg; Carbs 6g; Fiber 3g; Sugar 1g; Protein 5g

Eggs and Brussels Sprouts

Prep time: 10 minutes | Cook time: 4 hours | Serves: 4

4 eggs, mixed
Salt and black pepper to the taste
1 tablespoon avocado oil
2 shallots, minced
2 garlic cloves, minced
12 ounces Brussels sprouts, sliced
2 ounces bacon, chopped

1. Drizzle the oil on the bottom of slow cooker slow cooker and spread Brussels sprouts, garlic, bacon and shallots on the bottom. 2. Add Mixed eggs, salt and pepper, toss, cover and cook on Low temp setting for 4 hours. 3. serve right away for breakfast. Enjoy!

Per Serving: Calories 280; Fat 24g; Sodium 313mg; Carbs 14g; Fiber 4g; Sugar 6g; Protein 4g

Vegetable Quiche

Prep time: 10 minutes | Cook time: 20 minutes | Serves: 4

1 large carrot, shredded
1 large tomato, chopped
½ cup chopped kale
¼ cup almond milk
¼ onion, diced
½ bell pepper, diced
1 teaspoon basil
Pinch of pepper
¼ teaspoon paprika
8 eggs
1½ cups water

1. Pour the water into Instant Pot and lower the trivet. Place the eggs, almond milk, pepper, basil, and paprika, in a large bowl. Mix until smooth. Add the veggies to the mixture and stir well. Grease a baking dish with some cooking spray and pour the egg and veggie mixture into it. 2. Place the baking dish on top of the trivet and put the lid of the instant pot on. Press "MANUAL" and then set the cooking time to 20 minutes with the help of the "+" and "-" buttons. Cook on HIGH pressure. After the beep, press "KEEP WARM/CANCEL" and let the pressure come down on its own. Carefully open the lid once the pressure valve has dropped down. 3. Remove the quiche from the Instant Pot. Serve and enjoy!

Per Serving: Calories 174; Fat 14.6g; Sodium 51mg; Carbs 17.2g; Fiber 2.5g; Sugar 1.3g; Protein 9.8g

Mushroom Sliders

Prep time: 5 minutes | Cook time: 20 minutes | Serves: 3

3 Portobello mushroom caps
4 bacon slices
3 eggs
4 oz. smoked salmon

1. Heat up a pan over high heat, add bacon, cook until it's crispy. Place to paper towels and drain grease. 2. Heat up the pan with the bacon grease over heat and place egg rings in it. 3. Crack an egg in each, cook them for 6 minutes and place them to a plate. 4. Heat up the pan over high heat, add mushroom caps, cook the for 5 minutes and place them to a platter. Top each mushroom cap with bacon, salmon and eggs. Serve hot.

Per Serving: Calories 77; Fat 4.4g; Sodium 62mg; Carbs 0.6g; Fiber 0g; Sugar 0.6g; Protein 6.3g

Delicious Zucchini & Chicken Quiche

Prep time: 15 minutes | Cook time: 40 minutes | Serves: 5

For the Crust:

2 cups almond flour

1 pinch sea salt

1 large egg

2 tablespoon coconut oil

For the Filling:

Olive oil, for frying

1 lb. ground chicken

6 large eggs

1 teaspoon dried oregano

1 teaspoon fennel seed

1 teaspoon salt

½ teaspoon black pepper

½ cup heavy cream

1-2 zucchini, grated

1. Preheat oven to 350°F. Grease a pie dish (approx. 9inch dish) and set aside.

To prepare the crust: 1. Add the almond flour and salt to a food processor and pulse a few times to combine. 2. Add the egg and coconut oil and pulse until the mixture turns into a dough. Place to the prepared dish and press until distributed evenly.

To prepare the filling: 1. Heat some oil in a skillet, add the chicken and cook until lightly browned. When done, set aside to cool. 2. In a large bowl, beat the eggs, add the spices and cream and mix well. Mix in the chicken and zucchini and pour over the crust. 3. Bake in the preheated oven for about 30-40 minutes. When done, allow to cool slightly, slice and serve.

Per Serving: Calories 202; Fat 16.4g; Sodium 619mg; Carbs 2.3g; Fiber 0.3g; Sugar 0.9g; Protein 9.2g

Eggs Benedict

Prep time: 15 minutes | Cook time: 20 minutes | Serves: 2

The Bun:

3 pastured eggs

4 tablespoons unflavored egg white's

protein

Hollandaise:

6 egg yolks

4 tablespoons lemon juice

2 tablespoons mustard

1½ cups butter, melted

¼ teaspoon black pepper

1. Preheat and oven to 325°F and coat a baking sheet with cooking spray. Separate the egg yolks and egg whites in two different bowls. Using an electric mixer Mix the egg whites until fluffy. Slowly combine the mixed egg whites with the egg yolks and protein powder and stir until combined and become dough. Place the dough on the prepared baking sheet and bake for 20 minutes until golden brown. 2. Once it is done, remove from the oven and let it cool. After that, make the Hollandaise. Place the egg yolks, mustard, and lemon juice in a pan. Stir the three ingredients until mixed well. 3. Place the pan on the stove over a very low heat then bring to a simmer. Add melted butter into the pan and stir thoroughly. To assembly, cut the protein bun into halves horizontally. 4. Place the halved protein bun on a serving dish and top with sunny sides up. Pour the Hollandaise over the eggs and enjoy right away.

Per Serving: Calories 239; Fat 19.9g; Sodium 484mg; Carbs 0.6g; Fiber 0g; Sugar 0.1g; Protein 10.7g

Chapter 2 Vegetable and Sides Recipes

27	Easy Grilled Asparagus	32	Yummy Broccoli and Hazelnuts
27	Colorful Summer Vegetable Bake	33	Aromatic Dill Carrots
28	Mashed Coconut Pumpkin	33	Squash and Sweet Potato Soup
28	Zucchini Slaw	34	Simple Kale and Celery Dish
29	Spiced Broccoli	34	Vegetables Roast
29	Herbed Eggplant Slices	35	Herbed Spaghetti Squash
30	Savory Beans with Bacon	35	Healthy Cabbage, Carrot & Apple Stew
30	Zucchini with Scrambled Eggs	36	Tomato Gazpacho
31	Tasty Tuna Stuffed Tomatoes	36	Healthy Cabbage Slaw
31	Spiced Tofu and Zucchini Skewers	37	Baked Brussels Sprouts
32	Tomato Pasta with Basil	37	Onion Cucumber Salad

Easy Grilled Asparagus

Prep time: 5 minutes | Cook time: 23 minutes | Serves: 4

1-pound fresh asparagus spears, trimmed
1 tablespoon olive oil
salt and pepper to taste

1. Preheat grill to high heat. Coat asparagus spears lightly with olive oil. Season with pepper and salt to taste. Grill on high heat to desired tenderness for 23 minutes.

Per Serving: Calories 58; Fat 6.6g; Sodium 468mg; Carbs 7.7g; Fiber 2.4g; Sugar 4.4g; Protein 1.5g

Colorful Summer Vegetable Bake

Prep time: 10 minutes | Cook time: 1 hour | Serves: 4

⅓ cup extra virgin olive oil
1 clove garlic, sliced
4 tomatoes
3 small onions
1 summer squash
1 zucchini
1 teaspoon sea salt

1. Preheat to 400°F. In a small pan, heat the garlic and oil on high heat for about a minute, until the garlic starts to sizzle. Take it out of the heat and put in the side. 2. Slice the zucchini, squash, onions and tomatoes into ⅛-inch thick pieces. Set asides, alternate the slices of zucchini, squash, onion and tomato around the edge of a 9-inch deep dish glass pie pan or a similar sized round casserole dish in a circular pattern. Create a 2nd alternating circle in the middle. Tightly pack the vegetables. While baking, they will shrink. 3. Get rid of the garlic, if preferred, and drizzle oil on the vegetables. Sprinkle salt on top. 4. Let it bake for about an hour until the vegetables begin to brown and becomes tender. Allow it to cool for 10 minutes prior to serving.

Per Serving: Calories 303; Fat 22.4g; Sodium 558mg; Carbs 1.5g; Fiber 0.2g; Sugar 0.7g; Protein 20.2g

Mashed Coconut Pumpkin

Prep time: 5 minutes | Cook time: 35 minutes | Serves: 4

1 teaspoon. cinnamon powder
1 cup unsweetened coconut; shredded
1 pumpkin; peeled, seeded and cubed
½ cup coconut oil
A pinch of white pepper
A pinch of sea salt

1. Cook the pumpkin for 30 minutes. Drain water, add a pinch of salt and pepper, oil and coconut to the pan, stir and cook everything for 3 minutes more. 2. Mash using a potato masher, add cinnamon, stir well, cook for 2 minutes more, divide between plates and serve.

Per Serving: Calories 228; Fat 21.4g; Sodium 135mg; Carbs 1g; Fiber 0.3g; Sugar 0.2g; Protein 6.8g

Zucchini Slaw

Prep time: 35 minutes | Cook time: 0 minutes | Serves: 4

1½ pounds zucchini, grated
1 sweet onion, very thinly sliced
1½ teaspoons coarse kosher salt
1 small red bell pepper, diced
¼ cup cider vinegar
3 tablespoons frozen apple juice concentrate
2 tablespoons chopped fresh basil
Salt
Freshly ground pepper, to taste

1. Place onion and zucchini in a colander. Put in salt and toss to coat well. Allow to drain about a half hour. Rinse and squeeze vegetables. 2. Remove the squeezed vegetables to a bowl. Put in basil, apple juice concentrate, vinegar and bell pepper, then toss well. 3. Use pepper and salt to spiced then serve instantly.

Per Serving: Calories 58; Fat 6.6g; Sodium 468mg; Carbs 7.7g; Fiber 2.4g; Sugar 4.4g; Protein 1.5g

Spiced Broccoli

Prep time: 5 minutes | Cook time: 20 minutes | Serves: 3

2 cups broccoli florets
1 yellow bell pepper, sliced
1 tablespoon Montreal steak seasoning
2 teaspoons chili powder
1 teaspoon garlic powder
Salt and pepper to taste
1 tablespoon extra-virgin olive oil

1. Preheat oven to 400°F. In a bowl, mix the bell pepper and broccoli. Sprinkle pepper, salt, garlic powder, chili powder and steak seasoning on top of the vegetables and trickle it with olive oil, then toss until coated. 2. In a baking dish, spread the vegetables. Let it bake in the preheated oven for 15-20 minutes until the vegetables start to brown and become tender.

Per Serving: Calories 58; Fat 6.6g; Sodium 468mg; Carbs 7.7g; Fiber 2.4g; Sugar 4.4g; Protein 1.5g

Herbed Eggplant Slices

Prep time: 5 minutes | Cook time: 14 minutes | Serves: 3

1 clove garlic, minced
1 tablespoon minced fresh oregano
¼ cup chopped fresh basil
½ cup chopped fresh parsley
1 eggplant, sliced into ½ inch rounds
Salt to taste
Ground black pepper to taste

1. Set oven to 400°F. Use cooking spray to coat a baking tray. Add and mix parsley, basil, oregano, and garlic in a small bowl. Mix thoroughly then put aside. Spiced with pepper and salt on both sides of every eggplant slice. 2. Place to the baking tray. Bake until tender and lightly browned, about 5-7 minutes per side. On eggplant slices, sprinkle herb mixture; broil ½ minute under the broiler. Remove to a serving plate; serve right away.

Per Serving: Calories 303; Fat 22.4g; Sodium 558mg; Carbs 1.5g; Fiber 0.2g; Sugar 0.7g; Protein 20.2g

Savory Beans with Bacon

Prep time: 10 minutes | Cook time: 25 minutes | Serves: 2

1½ pounds fresh green beans, rinsed and trimmed

3 ounces coarsely chopped pancetta

1 shallot, thinly sliced

Salt and black pepper to taste

1. Bring lightly salted water in a big pot to a boil. Put in green beans and boil until just softened, about 3-4 minutes. Drain beans and plunge them into ice water promptly. Let beans sit in ice water until cold then drain well and set aside. 2. In a big skillet, cook pancetta on high heat until crispy then set aside. Lower heat to then stir into the pancetta fat with shallots and cook gently for 10 minutes, or until shallots have turned dark golden brown. 3. Put in the skillet with green beans and pancetta, then toss and cook for 2 minutes, or until warmed through. Spiced with pepper and salt to taste before serving.

Per Serving: Calories 216; Fat 14.9g; Sodium 528mg; Carbs 1.2g; Fiber 0.4g; Sugar 0.3g; Protein 17.3g

Zucchini with Scrambled Eggs

Prep time: 5 minutes | Cook time: 15 minutes | Serves: 3

1½ tablespoons olive oil

2 large zucchinis, cut into large chunks

Salt and ground black pepper to taste

2 large eggs

1 teaspoon water, or as desired

1. Heat oil on high heat in a skillet; sauté the zucchini for roughly 10 minutes till becoming soft. Use the black pepper and salt to Spiced the zucchini. 2. Whip eggs using a fork in a bowl; pour in the water and whip till evenly combined. 3. Add eggs on top of the zucchini; cook and Mix for roughly 5 minutes till the eggs become scrambled and not runny anymore. 4. Use the black pepper and salt to spiced the eggs and zucchini.

Per Serving: Calories 185; Fat 14.3g; Sodium 342mg; Carbs 2.8g; Fiber 0.6g; Sugar 1.8g; Protein 7.5g

Tasty Tuna Stuffed Tomatoes

Prep time: 10 minutes | Cook time: 0 minutes | Serves: 1

1 tomato, top cut off and insides scooped
2 teaspoons balsamic vinegar
5 ounces canned tuna, drained
1 tablespoon mozzarella, chopped
1 tablespoon green onion, chopped
1 tablespoon basil, chopped

1. In a bowl, Add and mix the tune with the vinegar, mozzarella, onion and basil and stir well. 2. Stuff the tomato with this mix and serve for lunch.

Per Serving: Calories 200; Fat 13.2g; Sodium 473mg; Carbs 13.4g; Fiber 5.5g; Sugar 1.6g; Protein 8.5g

Spiced Tofu and Zucchini Skewers

Prep time: 15 minutes | Cook time: 10 minutes | Serves: 6

14 oz. tofu, drained, pressed and cut into 1inch pieces
1 red bell pepper, cut into chunks
¼ teaspoon pepper
¼ teaspoon cayenne pepper
½ teaspoon turmeric
2 teaspoon ground cumin
2 teaspoons paprika
1 small zucchini, cut into chunks
2 garlic cloves, minced
2 tablespoon tomato paste
2 tablespoon lemon juice
1 cup unsweetened coconut milk
¾ teaspoon salt

1. Preheat the grill over -high heat. Add all ingredients into the mixing bowl and mix well. Cover bowl and place in fridge for 1 hour. 2. Place marinated tofu, bell pepper, and zucchini pieces on soaked wooden skewers. 3. Place tofu skewers on hot grill and cook for 10 minutes or until lightly golden brown. Serve and enjoy.

Per Serving: Calories 180; Fat 14g; Sodium 332mg; Carbs 5g; Fiber 2g; Sugar 1g; Protein 9g

Tomato Pasta with Basil

Prep time: 10 minutes | Cook time: 2 minutes | Serves: 4

½ cup tomato paste

4 cups zoodles

¼ cup coconut cream

2 garlic cloves, minced

¼ cup veggie broth

2 cups canned diced tomatoes

2 tablespoons chopped basil

1 teaspoon chopped parsley

1. Place all of the ingredients in Instant Pot. Stir well to Add and mix everything. Put the lid on and seal. 2. Select "MANUAL" after you hear the sealing chime and then set the cooking time to 2 minutes. Cook on HIGH. 3. When the timer goes off, hit "KEEP WARM/CANCEL" to turn the Instant Pot off. 4. Move the handle from "Sealing" to "Venting" for a quick pressure release and open the lid carefully. 5. Serve and enjoy!

Per Serving: Calories 96; Fat 5g; Sodium 451mg; Carbs 6g; Fiber 1g; Sugar 1g; Protein 4g

Yummy Broccoli and Hazelnuts

Prep time: 5 minutes | Cook time: 20 minutes | Serves: 4

1 tablespoon. olive oil

1 garlic clove; minced

1 lb. broccoli florets

⅓ cup hazelnuts

Black pepper to the taste

1. Heat up a pan with the oil over high heat, add hazelnuts, stir and cook for 5 minutes. Place hazelnuts to a bowl and leave them aside. 2. Heat up the pan over high heat, add broccoli and garlic, stir; cover and cook for 6 minutes more. Add hazelnuts and black pepper to the taste, stir; divide between plates and serve.

Per Serving: Calories 199; Fat 16g; Sodium 313mg; Carbs 9g; Fiber 6g; Sugar 1g; Protein 8g

Aromatic Dill Carrots

Prep time: 5 minutes | Cook time: 35 minutes | Serves: 4

1 tablespoon. coconut oil; melted
2 tablespoons dill; chopped
1 lb. baby carrots
1 tablespoon. honey
A pinch of black pepper

1. Boil carrots over high heat, cover and simmer for 30 minutes. 2. Drain well, put carrots in a bowl; add melted oil, black pepper, dill and honey, stir very well, divide between plates and serve.

Per Serving: Calories 200; Fat 18g; Sodium 178mg; Carbs 4g; Fiber 2g; Sugar 1g; Protein 7g

Squash and Sweet Potato Soup

Prep time: 15 minutes | Cook time: 15 minutes | Serves: 4

2 cups cubed squash
2 cups cubed sweet potatoes
2 tablespoon coconut oil
1 onion, diced
1 tablespoon coconut cream
3 cups veggie broth
Pinch of thyme

1. Turn the Instant Pot on and press the "SAUTE" button. Melt the coconut oil. Add the onion and cook until they become soft, 3 minutes. 2. Stir in the potatoes and squash and cook for an additional minute, or until they begin to 'sweat'. 3. Pour the broth over and stir in the thyme. Close the lid and turn it clockwise. When sealed, choose "MANUAL" and set the time to 10 minutes. Cook on HIGH. 4. Select "KEEP WARM/CANCEL" after the beep. Allow the valve to drop on its own for a natural pressure release. Open the lid carefully and stir in the coconut cream. 5. Serve immediately and enjoy!

Per Serving: Calories 349; Fat 1g; Sodium 236mg; Carbs 4g; Fiber 1g; Sugar 2g; Protein 0g

Simple Kale and Celery Dish

Prep time: 5 minutes | Cook time: 20 minutes | Serves: 4

2 celery stalks; chopped
5 cups kale; torn
1 small red bell pepper; chopped

3 tablespoons. water
1 tablespoon. coconut oil

1. Heat up a pan with the oil over high heat, add celery, stir and cook for 10 minutes. Add kale, water and bell pepper, stir and cook for 10 minutes more. serve really soon!

Per Serving: Calories 200; Fat 18g; Sodium 178mg; Carbs 4g; Fiber 2g; Sugar 1g; Protein 7g

Vegetables Roast

Prep time: 10 minutes | Cook time: 25 minutes | Serves: 4

1 cup eggplant, diced
4 mushroom, sliced
2 garlic cloves, minced
2 tablespoons parsley, chopped
3 tablespoons vinegar
8 small asparagus spears, ends removed

2 bell pepper, cut into strips
1 cup zucchini, sliced
¼ cup olive oil
½ teaspoon pepper
1 teaspoon salt

1. Preheat the oven to 375°F. In a large bowl, Mix oil, garlic, parsley, pepper, salt, and vinegar. Add vegetables in a bowl and toss well. 2. Place vegetables in an aluminum foil container and pour remaining marinade over vegetables. Seal container. Bake for 25 minutes. Spice with pepper and salt. Serve and enjoy.

Per Serving: Calories 143; Fat 11g; Sodium 289mg; Carbs 4g; Fiber 1g; Sugar 1g; Protein 9g

Herbed Spaghetti Squash

Prep time: 10 minutes | Cook time: 15 minutes | Serves: 4

- 4 cups spaghetti squash, cooked
- 2 tablespoons fresh parsley, chopped
- ½ teaspoon dried thyme
- ½ teaspoon dried rosemary
- ½ teaspoon garlic powder
- 2 tablespoons olive oil
- ½ teaspoon pepper
- ½ teaspoon sage
- 1 teaspoon salt

1. Preheat the oven to 350°F. Add all ingredients into the large bowl and mix well. 2. Place bowl mixture to the baking dish and cook for 15 minutes. Stir well and serve.

Per Serving: Calories 135; Fat 12g; Sodium 87mg; Carbs 12g; Fiber 3g; Sugar 1g; Protein 4g

Healthy Cabbage, Carrot & Apple Stew

Prep time: 10 minutes | Cook time: 20 minutes | Serves: 4

- 2 carrots, chopped
- ½ cabbage, chopped
- 1 apple, diced
- 1 onion, diced
- 1 tablespoon grated ginger
- 2 beets, chopped
- 4 cups veggie broth
- 2 tablespoon chopped parsley
- ½ teaspoon garlic salt
- ¼ teaspoon pepper

1. Place all of the ingredients in Instant Pot. Stir well to Add and mix everything and close the lid. Seal and then hit the "MANUAL" button. 2. Set the cooking time to 20 minutes and cook on HIGH pressure. 3. After you hear the beep, select "KEEP WARM/CANCEL". Move the pressure handle from "Sealing" to "Venting" for a quick pressure release and open the lid carefully. 4. Pour into serving bowls and serve immediately. Enjoy!

Per Serving: Calories 102; Fat 8g; Sodium 235mg; Carbs 5g; Fiber 1g; Sugar 1g; Protein 1g

Tomato Gazpacho

Prep time: 15 minutes | Cook time: 0 minutes | Serves: 4

2½ pounds large tomatoes (4-5), cored and cut into pieces
1 English cucumber, cut into chunks
1 red bell pepper, seeded and cut into pieces
1 large clove garlic, crushed
3 tablespoons plus 2 teaspoons extra-virgin olive oil, divided
2 tablespoons plus 1 teaspoon red wine vinegar, divided
1 teaspoon plus a pinch of salt, divided
½ teaspoon plus a pinch of ground pepper, divided
1 avocado
¼ cup chopped fresh basil

1. Slice a quarter cup each of bell pepper, cucumber, and tomatoes from the large pieces; put in a small bowl. Cover then set aside in the refrigerator. 2. In a blender, puree half a teaspoon pepper, the remaining tomatoes, a teaspoon of salt, bell pepper and cucumber with garlic, 2 tablespoon vinegar, and 3 tablespoon oil until smooth; work in 2 batches. Move to a big bowl; cover and refrigerate for at least two hours to two days until chilled. 3. Chop the avocado and mix with the saved chopped veggies just before serving; mix in a pinch each of pepper and salt, basil, a teaspoon vinegar and the remaining 2 teaspoon oil. 4. Place the gazpacho in bowls; add chopped veggie salad on top.

Per Serving: Calories 181; Fat 14g; Sodium 426mg; Carbs 14g; Fiber 5g; Sugar 7g; Protein 3g

Healthy Cabbage Slaw

Prep time: 5 minutes | Cook time: 0 minutes | Serves: 4

2 cups finely shredded green cabbage
½ cup thinly sliced red bell pepper
⅓ cup thinly sliced red onion
2 tablespoons spiced rice vinegar
2 tablespoons extra-virgin olive oil
¼ teaspoon salt
⅛ teaspoon freshly ground pepper

1. In a big bowl, Add and mix cabbage, onion, bell pepper, oil and vinegar. 2. Sprinkle with salt and pepper to taste. Toss to combine, then serve.

Per Serving: Calories 82; Fat 7g; Sodium 153mg; Carbs 4g; Fiber 1g; Sugar 2g; Protein 1g

Baked Brussels Sprouts

Prep time: 5 minutes | Cook time: 30 minutes | Serves: 4

¼ cup avocado oil
4 lbs. Brussels sprouts; cut in quarters
A pinch of sea salt
Black pepper to the taste

1. In a bowl; mix Brussels sprouts with oil, salt and pepper, toss to coat well, spread on a lined baking sheet, Put in the oven at 375°F and bake for 30 minutes. Divide between plates and serve as a Paleo side dish!

Per Serving: Calories 65; Fat 3.6g; Sodium 270mg; Carbs 7.2g; Fiber 1.5g; Sugar 4.4g; Protein 1.9g

Onion Cucumber Salad

Prep time: 20 minutes | Cook time: 0 minutes | Serves: 4

1 English cucumber (about 11 ounces)
½ sweet onion, preferably Vidalia
2 tablespoons rice vinegar
2 tablespoons chopped fresh dill
½ teaspoon sea salt
½ teaspoon ground pepper

1. Slice the cucumber thinly and put in a bowl. Chop the onion horizontally using mandolin. Put into the cucumber. Sprinkle with vinegar. 2. Put in pepper, salt and dill and mix gently until well combined. Let stand to marinate for 15 minutes. Blend gently again before enjoying.

Per Serving: Calories 12; Fat 0g; Sodium 184mg; Carbs 3g; Fiber 1g; Sugar 1g; Protein 1g

Chapter 3 Poultry Recipes

39 Italian-Style Turkey Breasts
39 Grilled Chicken with Refreshing Cucumber Radish Salsa
40 Grilled herbed Chicken
40 Spiced Chicken
41 Thai Chicken and Veggie Stew
41 Cheese Chicken Meatballs
42 Delicious Caprese Chicken
42 Delicious Pear and Goose
43 Cheesy Ranch Chicken with Bacon
43 Curried Chicken with Sweet Potatoes & Peas
44 Cheese and Tomatoes Stuffed Turkey
44 Spiced Whole Chicken
45 Prosciutto Wrapped Chicken Breasts
45 Herbed Garlicky Wings
46 Healthy Chicken Zucchini Cutlets
46 Chicken with Mushrooms
47 Sour Turkey Breasts
47 Stewed Chicken with Veggies
48 Juicy Chicken with Blueberry Lime Salsa
48 Turkey and Broccoli Balls
49 Chicken Tagine with Pomegranates Seeds

Italian-Style Turkey Breasts

Prep time: 10 minutes | Cook time: 2 hours | Serves: 6

1½ cups Italian dressing
Salt and black pepper, to taste
2 tablespoons butter
1 (2 pound) bone-in turkey breast
2 garlic cloves, minced

1. Preheat the oven to 350°F and grease a baking dish with butter. Mix minced garlic cloves, salt and black pepper and rub the turkey breast with this mixture. 2. Place turkey breast in the baking dish and top evenly with Italian dressing. 3. Bake for about 2 hours, coating with pan juices. Dish out and serve immediately.

Per Serving: Calories 432; Fat 22g; Sodium 623mg; Carbs 1g; Fiber 0g; Sugar 0g; Protein 48g

Grilled Chicken with Refreshing Cucumber Radish Salsa

Prep time: 10 minutes | Cook time: 10 minutes | Serves: 2

2 tablespoons extra-virgin olive oil, divided
½ teaspoon ground coriander
½ teaspoon salt, divided
½ teaspoon ground pepper, divided
4 "thin-cut" boneless, skinless chicken breasts or cutlets (4 ounces each), trimmed
½ cup finely diced seeded English cucumber
½ cup finely diced radishes
¼ cup finely chopped fresh mint
2 teaspoons rice vinegar

1. Set the grill to preheat to -high. In a small bowl, mix the ¼ teaspoon pepper, ¼ teaspoon salt, coriander and 1 tablespoon of oil, then brush it on both sides of the chicken. 2. Let the chicken grill for 8-10 minutes in total, flipping once, until an inserted instant-read thermometer in the thickest part reads 165°F. Or, let the chicken cook in a grill pan on medium high heat. 3. In the meantime, in a bowl, mix the vinegar, mint, radishes and cucumber with the leftover ¼ teaspoon pepper, ¼ teaspoon salt and 1 tablespoon of oil, then serve it with the chicken.

Per Serving: Calories 318; Fat 19g; Sodium 546mg; Carbs 4g; Fiber 0g; Sugar 2g; Protein 28g

Grilled herbed Chicken

Prep time: 15 minutes | Cook time: 15 minutes | Serves: 6

6 boneless chicken breast halves (about 1½ pounds total)

¼ cup olive oil

6 cloves garlic, minced

1 tablespoon lemon peel, finely shredded

2 teaspoons snipped fresh thyme

1 teaspoon snipped fresh rosemary

¼ teaspoon crushed red pepper

¼ teaspoon salt

⅛ teaspoon ground black pepper

Fresh thyme sprigs (optional)

Lemon wedges (optional)

1. Place the chicken to a resealable plastic bag and set in a bowl. For the marinade, mix oil, crushed red pepper, garlic, black pepper, lemon peel, rosemary, salt and thyme in a small bowl. Spread the marinade atop chicken. Seal the bag and flip to coat the chicken. Place in a fridge to marinate for about 2 to 4 hours and turn the bag often. 2. Drain the chicken and get rid of the marinade. Place the chicken onto the rack of an uncovered grill directly atop coals. Let it grill for about 12 to 15 minutes or until no pink color of chicken remains, flipping once halfway through grilling (165°F). 3. Stud with lemon wedges and fresh thyme sprigs if desired.

Per Serving: Calories 364; Fat 16g; Sodium 415mg; Carbs 3g; Fiber 1g; Sugar 1g; Protein 43g

Spiced Chicken

Prep time: 10 minutes | Cook time: 5 hours | Serves: 4

5 chicken drumsticks

A pinch of salt and black pepper

1 teaspoon cayenne pepper

4 teaspoons sweet paprika

2 teaspoons onion powder

2 teaspoons thyme, dried

2 teaspoons garlic powder

1. In a bowl, mix cayenne with salt, pepper, paprika, onion powder, thyme and garlic powder and stir. 2. Rub chicken with this spice mix, put them in slow cooker, cover and cook on Low temp setting for 5 hours. 3. Discard bones and serve chicken with a side salad.

Per Serving: Calories 284; Fat 16g; Sodium 177mg; Carbs 5g; Fiber 1g; Sugar 1g; Protein 30g

Thai Chicken and Veggie Stew

Prep time: 10 minutes | Cook time: 6 hours | Serves: 4

1 and ½ pounds chicken thighs, skinless, boneless and cut into chunks
½ cup butternut squash, chopped
1 cup broccoli florets
1 cup tomatoes, chopped
1 cup red bell pepper, chopped
14 ounces coconut milk
1 cup tomato sauce
1 teaspoon cumin, ground
2 teaspoons garlic powder
2 teaspoons ginger, grated
2 teaspoons coriander, ground
1 teaspoon cinnamon powder
1 cup water

1. In slow cooker, mix chicken thighs with squash, broccoli, tomatoes, red bell pepper, coconut milk, tomato sauce, cumin, garlic powder, ginger, coriander, cinnamon and water, cover and cook on Low temp setting for 6 hours. 2. Divide between bowls and serve.

Per Serving: Calories 255; Fat 10g; Sodium 475mg; Carbs 2g; Fiber 1g; Sugar 0g; Protein 34g

Cheese Chicken Meatballs

Prep time: 10 minutes | Cook time: 15 minutes | Serves: 3

1-pound ground chicken
Salt and ground black pepper, to taste
2 tablespoons plain yogurt
½ cup almond flour
¼ cup cheddar cheese, grated
¼ cup tomato paste more for serving
3 teaspoons cayenne pepper powder
1 egg

1. In a bowl, mix chicken meat with salt, pepper, yogurt, flour, cheddar cheese, tomato paste, cayenne pepper, egg, and stir well. 2. Shape 9 meatballs, place on a lined baking sheet, and bake at 500°F for 15 minutes. 3. Serve chicken meatballs with hot sauce on the side.

Per Serving: Calories 185; Fat 7g; Sodium 731mg; Carbs 1g; Fiber 0g; Sugar 0g; Protein 27g

Delicious Caprese Chicken

Prep time: 10 minutes | Cook time: 15 minutes | Serves: 4

1-pound chicken breasts, boneless and skinless
¼ cup balsamic vinegar
1 tablespoon extra-virgin olive oil
Kosher salt and black pepper, to taste
4 mozzarella cheese slices

1. Spiced the chicken with salt and black pepper. Heat the olive oil in a skillet over medium heat and cook chicken for about 5 minutes per side. 2. Stir in the balsamic vinegar and cook for about 2 minutes. 3. Add mozzarella cheese slices and cook for about 2 minutes until melted. 4. Dish out in a plate and serve hot.

Per Serving: Calories 237; Fat 15g; Sodium 469mg; Carbs 2g; Fiber 1g; Sugar 1g; Protein 22g

Delicious Pear and Goose

Prep time: 10 minutes | Cook time: 28 minutes | Serves: 6

1 cup chicken broth
1 tablespoon ghee
½ cup slice onions
1½ pounds goose, chopped into large pieces
2 tablespoons balsamic vinegar
1 teaspoon cayenne pepper
3 pears, peeled and sliced
¼ teaspoon garlic powder
½ teaspoon pepper

1. Turn the Instant Pot on and set it to "SAUTE". Add the ghee. When melted, add the goose and cook until it becomes golden on all sides. Place to a plate. Add the onions and cook for 2 minutes. 2. Return the goose to the pot and add the rest of the ingredients. Stir well to combine and close the lid. Turn it clockwise so it is sealed properly. Select the "MANUAL" cooking mode. 3. Set the cooking time to 18 minutes. Cook on HIGH pressure. When the timer goes off, press the "KEEP WARM/CANCEL" button. 4. Move the pressure handle from "Sealing" to "Venting" for a quick pressure release. Serve and enjoy!

Per Serving: Calories 355; Fat 25g; Sodium 647mg; Carbs 11g; Fiber 2g; Sugar 0.6g; Protein 22g

Cheesy Ranch Chicken with Bacon

Prep time: 10 minutes | Cook time: 25 minutes | Serves: 4

4 boneless skinless chicken breasts
4 slices thick cut bacon, cooked and crisped
Kosher salt and black pepper, to taste
1½ cups mozzarella cheese, shredded
2 teaspoons ranch spicing

1. Preheat the oven to 390°F and grease a baking dish. Spiced the chicken breasts with kosher salt and black pepper. Cook chicken breasts in a nonstick skillet for about 5 minutes per side. 2. Top the chicken with mozzarella cheese and ranch spicing and place to the oven. 3. Bake for about 15 minutes and dish out on a platter. Crumble the crispy bacon and sprinkle over the chicken to serve.

Per Serving: Calories 416; Fat 26g; Sodium 666mg; Carbs 0g; Fiber 0g; Sugar 0g; Protein 36g

Curried Chicken with Sweet Potatoes & Peas

Prep time: 10 minutes | Cook time: 4 hours | Serves: 2

3 cups cubed peeled sweet potatoes
1 cup chopped onion
2 tablespoons curry powder
2 tablespoons minced fresh ginger
6 cloves garlic, minced
2 pounds bone in, skinless chicken thighs (4 thighs)
½ teaspoon kosher salt
2 teaspoons olive oil
1 cup chopped red or orange bell pepper
1 cup sugar snap peas, halved
1 (14 ounce) can unsweetened light coconut milk
¼ cup fresh cilantro
1 lime, cut into 4 wedges

1. In a 4 to 5-quart slow cooker, mix the garlic, ginger, curry powder, onion and sweet potatoes. Sprinkle salt on the chicken, then add it to the slow cooker. 2. Trickle with oil. Put cover and let it cook for 3 to 3½ hours on High, until the chicken reads at least 165°F using an instant-read thermometer. 3. Add the coconut milk, snap peas and bell pepper into the slow cooker. 4. Put cover and let it cook for about 10 more minutes on High until heated through. Put cilantro on top and serve it with lime wedges.

Per Serving: Calories 319; Fat 22g; Sodium 430mg; Carbs 1g; Fiber 0g; Sugar 0g; Protein 29g

Cheese and Tomatoes Stuffed Turkey

Prep time: 15 minutes | Cook time: 1 hour 15 minutes | Serves: 2

1 tablespoon butter
2 large turkey breasts
½ cup fresh mozzarella cheese, thinly sliced
Salt and black pepper, to taste
1 large Roma tomato, thinly sliced

1. Preheat the oven to 375°F and grease the baking tray with butter. Make some deep slits in the turkey breasts and spice with salt and black pepper. 2. Stuff the mozzarella cheese slices and tomatoes in the turkey slits. 3. Put the stuffed turkey breasts on the baking tray and place to the oven. Bake for about 1 hour 15 minutes and dish out to serve warm.

Per Serving: Calories 222; Fat 12g; Sodium 472mg; Carbs 1g; Fiber 1.7g; Sugar 3.6g; Protein 25g

Spiced Whole Chicken

Prep time: 10 minutes | Cook time: 25 minutes | Serves: 8

3-pound whole chicken
1 cup chicken broth
1½ tablespoons olive oil
1 teaspoon paprika
¾ teaspoon garlic powder
¼ teaspoon onion powder

1. Rinse the chicken well under cold water, remove the giblets, and pat it dry with some paper towels. In a small bowl, Add and mix the oil and spices. Rub the chicken well with the mixture. Turn Instant Pot on and set it to "SAUTE". 2. Add the chicken to it and sear on all sides until it becomes golden. Pour the chicken broth around the chicken (not over it), and put the lid on. seal and press the "MANUAL" button. Set the cooking time to 25 minutes and cook on HIGH pressure. 3. When the timer goes off, select "KEEP WARM/CANCEL". Move the pressure handle from "Sealing" to "Venting" for a quick pressure release. Place the chicken to a platter and let sit for about 10 minutes before carving. 4. Serve and enjoy!

Per Serving: Calories 306; Fat 17g; Sodium 435mg; Carbs 1g; Fiber 0g; Sugar 0g; Protein 34g

Prosciutto Wrapped Chicken Breasts

Prep time: 10 minutes | Cook time: 35 minutes | Serves: 4

4 chicken breasts, boneless and skinless
4 oz. Boursin cheese
4 prosciutto slices
Kosher salt and black pepper, to taste
½ cup mozzarella cheese, shredded

1. Preheat the oven to 400°F and grease a baking dish. 2. Spiced the chicken with salt and black pepper and top with Boursin and mozzarella cheese. Wrap chicken breasts with prosciutto slices and Place into a baking dish. 3. Put in the oven and bake for about 35 minutes. Remove from the oven and serve hot.

Per Serving: Calories 140; Fat 6g; Sodium 184mg; Carbs 0g; Fiber 0g; Sugar 0g; Protein 20g

Herbed Garlicky Wings

Prep time: 15 minutes | Cook time: 10 minutes | Serves: 4

12 chicken wings
¼ cup chicken broth
1 tablespoon basil
1 tablespoon oregano
½ tablespoon tarragon
1 tablespoon minced garlic
2 tablespoons olive oil
¼ teaspoon pepper
1 cup of water

1. Pour the water into the Instant Pot and lower the rack. Place all of the ingredients in a bowl and mix well. Cover the bowl and let the wings sit for about 15 minutes. 2. Place on the rack and close the lid of the Instant Pot. Turn it clockwise until you hear the chime that indicates proper sealing. Select the "MANUAL" button and with the "+" and "-" buttons set the cooking time to 10 minutes. Cook on HIGH. After the beep, select "KEEP WARM/CANCEL". 3. Move the pressure handle from "Sealing" to "Venting" in order to do a quick pressure release. 4. Serve the wings drizzled with the cooking liquid and enjoy!

Per Serving: Calories 182; Fat 12g; Sodium 538mg; Carbs 1g; Fiber 1g; Sugar 0g; Protein 16g

Healthy Chicken Zucchini Cutlets

Prep time: 5 minutes | Cook time: 6 minutes | Serves: 6

3 zucchinis, boiled and mashed
3 tablespoons lemon pepper spicing
½ pound chicken, boiled and chopped
½ cup avocado oil
Salt and black pepper, to taste

1. Mix chicken, zucchinis, lemon pepper spicing, salt and black pepper in a bowl. 2. Make cutlets out of this mixture and set aside. Heat avocado oil in a pan and put the cutlets in it. 3. Fry for about 2-3 minutes on each side and dish out to serve.

Per Serving: Calories 243; Fat 18g; Sodium 368mg; Carbs 0g; Fiber 0g; Sugar 0g; Protein 19g

Chicken with Mushrooms

Prep time: 10 minutes | Cook time: 30 minutes | Serves: 6

2 pounds' chicken breasts, cubed
4 tablespoons ghee
1¼ pounds mushrooms, sliced
½ cup chicken broth
2 tablespoons arrowroot
½ cup almond milk
¼ teaspoon black pepper
2 leeks, sliced
¼ teaspoon garlic powder

1. Turn Instant Pot on and set it to "SAUTE". Add the ghee and wait until it is melted. 2. Place the chicken cubes inside and cook until they are no longer pink and become slightly golden in color. Place the chicken pieces to a plate. Add the leeks and sliced mushrooms to the pot and cook for about 3 minutes. Return the chicken to the Instant Pot, Spiced Spice with pepper and garlic powder and pour the broth over. 3. Give the mixture a good stir and mix everything well, then close the lid. Seal and then hit the "MANUAL" button. Set the cooking time to 8 minutes and cook on HIGH pressure. After the beeping sound, hit "KEEP WARM/CANCEL". Move the pressure handle from "Sealing" to "Venting" to release the pressure quickly. 4. In a bowl, Mix the almond milk and arrowroot. Pour the mixture over the chicken and set the Instant Pot to "SAUTE" again. Cook until the sauce becomes thickened. 5. Serve and enjoy!

Per Serving: Calories 419; Fat 28g; Sodium 699mg; Carbs 12g; Fiber 4g; Sugar 2g; Protein 28g

Sour Turkey Breasts

Prep time: 15 minutes | Cook time: 25 minutes | Serves: 3

½ onion, chopped
2 garlic cloves, minced
1 pound pastured turkey breasts
½ cup sour cream
Salt and black pepper, to taste

1. Preheat the grill to high heat. Mix sour cream, onion, garlic, salt and black pepper in a bowl. 2. Add turkey breasts to this mixture and marinate for about an hour. Place the marinated turkey breasts to the grill. Grill for about 25 minutes and transfer to a plate to serve.

Per Serving: Calories 285; Fat 16g; Sodium 497mg; Carbs 1g; Fiber 0g; Sugar 1g; Protein 34g

Stewed Chicken with Veggies

Prep time: 10 minutes | Cook time: 15 minutes | Serves: 8

1-pound ground chicken
1 cup chopped tomatoes
1 cup diced onions
1 cup chopped carrots
1 cup chopped kale
½ cup chopped celery
6 cups chicken broth
2 thyme sprigs
1 tablespoon olive oil
1 teaspoon red pepper flakes
10 ounces potato noodles

1. Turn the Instant Pot on and set it to "SAUTE". Add the oil and cook until it becomes hot and sizzling. Add the chicken and cook until it becomes golden. Stir in the onions, carrots, and celery, and cook for about 5 minutes. Stir in the remaining ingredients, except the noodles, and close the lid. Select the "MANUAL" cooking mode. Set the cooking time to 6 minutes. Cook on HIGH pressure. 2. When the timer goes off, press the "KEEP WARM/CANCEL" button. Move the pressure handle from "Sealing" to "Venting" for a quick pressure release and open the lid carefully. 3. Stir in the potato noodles and close the lid again. Seal and click on "MANUAL" again. This time, cook for 4 minutes on HIGH. 4. Again, press "KEEP WARM/CANCEL" after the beep and do a quick pressure release. Open the lid and ladle into serving bowls. Enjoy!

Per Serving: Calories 358; Fat 25g; Sodium 896mg; Carbs 8g; Fiber 3g; Sugar 2g; Protein 25g

Juicy Chicken with Blueberry Lime Salsa

Prep time: 10 minutes | Cook time: 24 minutes | Serves: 2

1 lime
1 tablespoon canola oil
¼ teaspoon salt plus ⅛ teaspoon, divided
¼ teaspoon ground pepper
2 bone-in, skinless chicken breasts, cut in half crosswise
1 cup blueberries, fresh or frozen (thawed), coarsely chopped if large
½ serrano or jalapeño pepper, or to taste, finely chopped
2 tablespoons finely chopped shallot
1 tablespoon chopped fresh cilantro

1. In a small bowl, mix pepper, ¼ teaspoon of salt, oil and zest. In a dish, Place chicken, meat-side up; top with the mixture. Put into the refrigerator with a cover for a minimum of 2 hours up to 8 hours. Turn on the grill to preheat. 2. Use oil to grease grill rack. Put chicken on grill for 8-12 minutes on each side until an instant-read thermometer reaches 165°F when inserted into the thickest part but do not touch the bone. On a serving plate, place cooked chicken and allow to rest for 5 minutes. 3. At the same time, cut off the reserved lime ends. Take out and discard white pith using a sharp knife. Cut segments from surrounding membranes; chop coarsely. 4. In a small mixing bowl, mix chopped lime, the remaining ⅛ teaspoon salt, cilantro, shallot, chile and blueberries; gently stir. 5. Serve with chicken.

Per Serving: Calories 164; Fat 8g; Sodium 397mg; Carbs 5g; Fiber 0g; Sugar 0g; Protein 16g

Turkey and Broccoli Balls

Prep time: 5 minutes | Cook time: 20 minutes | Serves: 6

1 cup broccoli, chopped
1-pound turkey, boiled and chopped
2 teaspoons ginger-garlic paste
Salt and lemon pepper spicing, to taste
½ cup olive oil

1. Preheat the oven to 360°F and grease a baking tray. 2. Mix turkey, olive oil, broccoli, ginger-garlic paste, salt and lemon pepper spicing in a bowl. Make small balls out of this mixture and place on the baking tray. 3. Transfer to the oven and bake for about 20 minutes. 4. Remove from the oven and serve with the dip of choice.

Per Serving: Calories 156; Fat 7g; Sodium 404mg; Carbs 1g; Fiber 0g; Sugar 0g; Protein 21g

Chicken Tagine with Pomegranates Seeds

Prep time: 10 minutes | Cook time: 50 minutes | Serves: 2

1¼ cups fresh pearl onions, or frozen small whole onions
1 tablespoon extra-virgin olive oil
1 teaspoon ground ginger
⅛ teaspoon freshly ground pepper
1¼ pounds boneless, skinless chicken thighs, trimmed
1½ cups pomegranate juice
¾ cup pitted prunes
½ cup dried apricots
15 sprigs cilantro, tied with kitchen string
½ teaspoon salt
2 tablespoons sesame seeds, for garnish
1 cup pomegranate seeds, for garnish

1. Preheat oven to 350°F. Cook pearl onions in boiling water for 1 minute if using fresh ones. Drain. When cool enough to handle, peel. Or rinse under warm water to thaw in case you use frozen onions. 2. In a Dutch oven, heat oil over -high heat. Put in pepper and ginger; cook for around 1 minute, stirring, till beginning to foam and fragrant. Add chicken and onions; coat by stirring. Cook for nearly 5 to 8 minutes till onions begin to turn golden, stirring. Add prunes, pomegranate juice, cilantro, apricots, and salt; bring to a simmer. Use foil to cover tightly and then with a lid. Place into the oven and bake for 30 minutes. 3. Take away lid and remove foil. Discard cilantro. Return to oven and uncover while baking for an addition of 10 minutes till the chicken is tender and cooked through. 4. In the meantime, in a small dry skillet, toast sesame seeds over low heat for around 2 to 3 minutes till fragrant and light golden, stirring constantly. Place into a small bowl in order to cool the seed. 5. When serving, spoon the tagine onto plates or into serving bowl. Add pomegranate seeds and sesame seeds for garnishing.

Per Serving: Calories 316; Fat 22g; Sodium 720mg; Carbs 0g; Fiber 0g; Sugar 0g; Protein 29g

Chapter 4 Beef, Pork, and Lamb Recipes

51	Spicy Barbecued Spareribs	56	Pork in Wine Marinade
51	Aromatic Cinnamon Pork Chops	56	Garlicky Roast Lamb Leg
52	Juicy Pork Chops	57	Delicious Citrusy Beef
52	Crispy Pork Roast	57	Tangy Pork Chops and Mushrooms
53	Hot Barbequed Steak	58	Traditional Beef Ragu
53	Spicy Cajun Roast Beef	58	Teriyaki Pork Ribs
54	Smoky Baby Back Ribs	59	Lime Pork Tenderloin with Kale
54	Tangy Apple Pork Ribs	59	Grilled T-Bone Steaks
55	Pork Roast with Yucca	60	Pineapple Pork Roast
55	Mexican-style Beef Stew	60	Pulled Pork with Barbeque Sauce

Spicy Barbecued Spareribs

Prep time: 5 minutes | Cook time: 60 minutes | Serves: 2

1 (4 pound) package pork spareribs, rinsed and patted dry

Salt and ground black pepper to taste

1 cup water

1 cup sweet chili sauce

1. Prepare the oven by preheating to 350°F. Season the spareribs with pepper and salt. Add the water into the bottom of a large baking dish then lay the spareribs in the dish; use aluminum foil to cover. 2. Place in the preheated oven and bake for 30 minutes; add about half the chili sauce on top of the meat, cover, and put back to the oven. 3. Every 5 minutes, sweep the ribs with more chili sauce and keep on cooking for 30 minutes until the meat pulls away simply from the bone. 4. Serve cold or hot.

Per Serving: Calories 574; Fat 40.4g; Sodium 557mg; Carbs 9.6g; Fiber 1.7g; Sugar 6.3g; Protein 32.7g

Aromatic Cinnamon Pork Chops

Prep time: 10 minutes | Cook time: 10 minutes | Serves: 4

2 tablespoons ghee

A pinch of salt and black pepper

4 pork chops, boneless

2 tablespoons stevia

A pinch of nutmeg, ground

1 tablespoon apple cider vinegar

1 teaspoon cinnamon powder

1. Heat up a pan with the ghee over -high heat, add pork chops and cook them for 5 minutes. Flip the chops, spiced them with salt, pepper, stevia, nutmeg and cinnamon, drizzle the vinegar and cook for 5 minutes more. 2. Divide the chops between plates and serve for lunch. Enjoy!

Per Serving: Calories 441; Fat 37g; Sodium 745mg; Carbs 4g; Fiber 1g; Sugar 2g; Protein 22g

Juicy Pork Chops

Prep time: 10 minutes | Cook time: 15 minutes | Serves: 2

4 (5 ounce) boneless center-cut pork chops, ½inch thick

¼ teaspoon salt

¼ teaspoon cracked black pepper

2 tablespoons butter, divided

1 large orange

1 tablespoon chopped fresh sage leaves

1. Season the chops with cracked black pepper and salt. Melt 1 tablespoon butter over -high heat in a big nonstick skillet, then cook chops for 8 minutes, flipping once, until done. 2. In the meantime, grate 1 teaspoon peel, then squeeze ¼ cup of orange juice. Place the chops to a serving platter, then keep them warm. 3. Melt the leftover 1 tablespoon butter, spread in the same skillet over high heat. Put in orange juice, then boil, scraping the brown bits from the pan's bottom. Boil until the mixture reduces slightly, 1 minute. 4. Discard from the heat, then mix in orange peel and sage. Drizzle over the chops.

Per Serving: Calories139; Fat 5.8g; Sodium 467mg; Carbs 7.1g; Fiber 2.6g; Sugar 3.5g; Protein 12.8g

Crispy Pork Roast

Prep time: 10 minutes | Cook time: 1-1½ hours | Serves: 6

1 tablespoon dill seed

1 tablespoon fennel seed

1 teaspoon dried oregano

1 teaspoon lemon pepper

¼ teaspoon onion powder

¼ teaspoon garlic powder

4 pounds' boneless pork roast

1. Preheat an oven to 325°F. Mix garlic powder, onion powder, lemon pepper, oregano, fennel seed and dill seed in small bowl; stir well and apply to the roast. 2. Put roast in a 10x15inch roasting pan. 3. Bake for 1-1½ hours at 325°F till internal pork temperature reaches 145°F.

Per Serving: Calories 338; Fat 18g; Sodium 788mg; Carbs 14g; Fiber 5g; Sugar 2g; Protein 28g

Hot Barbequed Steak

Prep time: 5 minutes | Cook time: 15 minutes | Serves: 2

4 (½ pound) beef top sirloin steaks
½ cup vegetable oil
1-ounce steak spice seasoning mix

1. Place steak spice and oil on a platter big enough to fit the steaks. 2. Coat the steak evenly with spices and oil. Turn an outdoor grill to high heat and lightly grease the grate. 3. Grill the steaks over high heat on the preheated grill until reach your desired doneness.

Per Serving: Calories 340; Fat 20.3g; Sodium 851mg; Carbs 5.6g; Fiber 1.5g; Sugar 1.8g; Protein 26.4g

Spicy Cajun Roast Beef

Prep time: 15 minutes | Cook time: 8-10 hours | Serves: 2

2 teaspoons garlic, minced
½ teaspoon prepared horseradish
1 teaspoon hot pepper sauce
1 teaspoon dried thyme
½ teaspoon salt
½ teaspoon ground black pepper
2 teaspoons Cajun spicing
2 tablespoons olive oil
2 tablespoons malt vinegar
2 pounds' beef eye of round roast

1. In a bowl, mix malt vinegar, olive oil, Cajun spicing, pepper, salt, thyme, hot pepper sauce, horseradish, and garlic. Use a meat fork to pierce all over the beef roast. 2. In a big resealable plastic bag, put the roast. Add the marinade and flip the roast to thoroughly coat. Chill overnight, flipping sometimes if you want. 3. Once ready to cook, in a slow cooker, put the roast with the leftover marinade. Do not add water. Roast on Low until reaching the doneness you want, about 8-10 hours. 4. A meat thermometer should display 135°F for rare. Take out of the slow cooker to a serving dish and let sit before cutting across the grain, about 15 minutes.

Per Serving: Calories 421; Fat 23.4g; Sodium 990mg; Carbs 4.8g; Fiber 1.3g; Sugar 1.2g; Protein 39.5g

Smoky Baby Back Ribs

Prep time: 10 minutes | Cook time: 3 hours | Serves: 2

2 tablespoons garlic powder
2 tablespoons onion powder
1 tablespoon fine sea salt
1 tablespoon ground black pepper
1 rack baby back pork ribs
1 (6x18inch) cedar plank
¾ cup barbeque sauce, or to taste

1. In a small bowl, add and mix salt, black pepper, onion powder and garlic powder. Scatter on baby back ribs. Cover using plastic wrap and chill for 8 hours up to overnight. 2. On a rimmed baking sheet, put the plank and add in sufficient water to submerge. Allow to soak for an hour prior to grilling. Let drain. 3. Preheat the outdoor grill to 500°F. On grate, set the plank and heat for 5 minutes till slightly charred. Turn the plank and set the ribs over. 4. Reduce the heat and place cover on the grill. Let the ribs cook for 3 hours, drizzling some water over after every half an hour to make steam in the grill, till soft. 5. Remove the grill cover and raise the heat to high. Brush top of ribs with barbeque sauce. Allow to cook for 2 minutes till ribs turn dark brown.

Per Serving: Calories 476; Fat 33.5g; Sodium 860mg; Carbs 4.3g; Fiber 1.3g; Sugar 1.3g; Protein 29.9g

Tangy Apple Pork Ribs

Prep time: 10 minutes | Cook time: 30 minutes | Serves: 4

½ cup apple cider vinegar
2 pounds' pork ribs
3½ cups apple juice

1. Pour the apple juice and the apple cider vinegar into the Instant Pot and lower the trivet. 2. Place the pork ribs on top of the trivet and then close the lid. seal properly. After the chime, choose the "MANUAL" cooking mode. Set the cooking time to 30 minutes. Cook on HIGH pressure. 3. After the beep, press the "KEEP WARM/CANCEL" button. Let the valve drop on its own for a natural pressure release. Serve.

Per Serving: Calories 530; Fat 43g; Sodium 866mg; Carbs 2g; Fiber 0.5g; Sugar 23g; Protein 32g

Pork Roast with Yucca

Prep time: 10 minutes | Cook time: 90 minutes | Serves: 2

8 cloves garlic, peeled
¼ cup salt
¼ cup black pepper
2 teaspoons chopped fresh oregano
3 tablespoons olive oil
1 (10 pound) pork picnic roast
4 yucca (cassava) roots, peeled and sliced

1. Preheat the oven to 425°F. In a blender or food processor's container, insert the olive oil, oregano, pepper, salt and garlic before processing until smoothened. Create a few incisions in pork roast with a small knife. 2. Use a little spoon to put garlic paste into each incision. In a roaster, insert pork before covering up. Put it into the preheated oven, baking for 90 minutes. 3. During the process, check on it about every 15 minutes. It is ready when the internal temperature reads 175°F. As the meat roasts, put yucca into a big pot filled with water that's boiling. Continue cooking until the yucca tenderizes and is easily cut with a fork. Put together with pork roast before serving.

Per Serving: Calories 442; Fat 29.8g; Sodium 575mg; Carbs 2.4g; Fiber 0.4g; Sugar 1.1g; Protein 29.8g

Mexican-style Beef Stew

Prep time: 10 minutes | Cook time: 8 hours | Serves: 4

1-pound beef stew meat, cubed
3 tomatoes, roughly chopped
1 red onion, chopped
1 garlic clove, minced
5 ounces canned green chilies, chopped
2 teaspoons chili powder
1 teaspoon cumin powder
1 teaspoon oregano, dried
2 cups water
2 cups beef stock
A pinch of salt and black pepper

1. Put meat in slow cooker. Add tomatoes, onion, garlic, chilies, chili powder, cumin powder, oregano, water, stock, salt and pepper, cover and cook on Low temp setting for 8 hours. 2. Divide between bowls and serve. Enjoy!

Per Serving: Calories 507; Fat 42g; Sodium 1201mg; Carbs 3g; Fiber 1g; Sugar 2g; Protein 29g

Pork in Wine Marinade

Prep time: 5 minutes | Cook time: 15 minutes | Serves: 2

2 tablespoons olive oil
1½ pounds pork tenderloin, cut into bite-size pieces
2 cloves garlic, minced
4 sprigs fresh cilantro, chopped
3 tablespoons olive oil
4 tablespoons red wine vinegar
2 tablespoons port wine
1 pinch salt
1 pinch black pepper
1 pinch cayenne pepper

1. In a big, heavy skillet, heat 2 tablespoons olive oil over high heat. Sauté pork until cooked through and turning brown evenly. Remove to a bowl and sprinkle garlic and cilantro over; keep warm. 2. Mix port, vinegar, and 3 tablespoons olive oil in a small bowl. Use cayenne, black pepper, and salt to season. Stir until reaching a creamy consistency. 3. Mix into the cooked pork and enjoy immediately.

Per Serving: Calories 429; Fat 27.3g; Sodium 836mg; Carbs 6.6g; Fiber 3.4g; Sugar 1.9g; Protein 29.2g

Garlicky Roast Lamb Leg

Prep time: 15 minutes | Cook time: 2 hours | Serves: 2

4 cloves garlic, sliced
2 tablespoons fresh rosemary
Salt to taste
Ground black pepper to taste
5 pounds' leg of lamb

1. Set oven to 350°F to preheat. Make slits every 3 to 4 inches over top of the lamb's leg, deep enough to push slices of garlic down into the meat. Liberally sprinkle pepper and salt over top of lamb to season; place several fresh rosemary sprigs over top and bottom of the lamb. 2. Position lamb on a roasting pan. Roast lamb for about 1¾ to 2 hours in preheated oven until desired doneness is reached. Do not overcook the lamb. Keep the lamb meat slightly pink for the best flavor. 3. Allow meat to stand for at least 10 minutes before cutting to serve.

Per Serving: Calories 531; Fat 29g; Sodium 1036mg; Carbs 6g; Fiber 2g; Sugar 2g; Protein 50g

Delicious Citrusy Beef

Prep time: 15 minutes | Cook time: 75 minutes | Serves: 6

Juice of 1 lemon
Juice of 2 oranges
2 pounds' beef, cut into chunks
1 tablespoon ghee
1 tablespoon seasoning by choice
½ teaspoon sea salt

1. Place the beef in the Instant Pot and sprinkle with salt, pepper, and seasoning. Massage the meat with hands to season it well. Pour the lemon and orange juice over and then put the lid on. Seal it. 2. Select "MANUAL" and set the cooking time to 50 minutes. Cook on HIGH pressure. 3. When the timer goes off, turn the pressure handle to "Venting" for a quick pressure release and open the lid carefully. Shred the meat inside the pot with two forks. 4. Keep the lid open and set the Instant Pot to SAUTE. Stir to Add and mix and sauté for about 20 minutes, or until the liquid is absorbed. 5. Add the ghee, give the mixture a good stir, and cook for additional 5 minutes. Serve and enjoy!

Per Serving: Calories 539; Fat 43g; Sodium 861mg; Carbs 7g; Fiber 2g; Sugar 1g; Protein 30g

Tangy Pork Chops and Mushrooms

Prep time: 15 minutes | Cook time: 90 minutes | Serves: 2

4 thick cut pork chops, boneless
Salt and pepper to taste
10 ounces fresh mushrooms, sliced
1 onion
1 (14 ounce) can stewed tomatoes, with juice

1. Set the oven to 350°F to preheat. Cut onion into thick slices and place them on the bottom of a casserole dish. Lay over the onions with pork chops, then season with pepper and salt. 2. Use mushrooms to cover the chops and drizzle over all with stewed tomatoes. Bake at 350°F with a cover for about an hour. 3. Take off the cover and bake for half an hour.

Per Serving: Calories 500; Fat 39g; Sodium 996mg; Carbs 5g; Fiber 2g; Sugar 2g; Protein 33g

Traditional Beef Ragu

Prep time: 10 minutes | Cook time: 45 minutes | Serves: 5

18 ounces beef

2 bay leaves

5 garlic cloves, crushed

7 ounces jarred roasted red peppers, chopped

28 ounces canned crushed tomatoes

1 tablespoon chopped parsley

½ tablespoon olive oil

1 teaspoon sea salt

½ teaspoon black pepper

1. Season the beef with salt and pepper. Turn the Instant Pot on and set it to "SAUTE". Add the oil to it and wait until it becomes hot. Place the beef inside and cook until the meat becomes browned on all sides. 2. Add the rest of the ingredients and give the mixture a good stir. Close the lid and turn clockwise to seal. 3. Select the "MANUAL" mode. Set the time to 45 minutes. Cook on HIGH pressure. Select "KEEP WARM/CANCEL" after the beeping sound. Wait for the valve to drop on its own for a natural pressure release. Open the lid carefully and serve.

Per Serving: Calories 441; Fat 34g; Sodium 788mg; Carbs 11g; Fiber 4g; Sugar 2g; Protein 25g

Teriyaki Pork Ribs

Prep time: 30 minutes | Cook time: 2 hours | Serves: 2

2 pounds country style pork ribs

4 cups chicken broth

⅛ cup teriyaki sauce

1½ tablespoons garlic powder

1 tablespoon onion powder

Salt and pepper to taste

1. Place the ribs in a roasting pan. Mix the teriyaki sauce, onion powder, salt, chicken broth, garlic powder, and pepper. Pour the mixture all over the ribs. Cover the pan and marinate the ribs for ½ hour. 2. Set the oven to 350°F to preheat. Use an aluminum foil to cover the roasting pan. 3. Place the pan in the oven and roast it for 2 hours until the meat is tender enough that it easily falls off the bone. 4. Check it to ensure that the juices won't boil over into the oven; if necessary, discard some broth from the pan.

Per Serving: Calories 396; Fat 28g; Sodium 456mg; Carbs 2g; Fiber 0g; Sugar 0g; Protein 34g

Lime Pork Tenderloin with Kale

Prep time: 5 minutes | Cook time: 60 minutes | Serves: 2

2 limes, juiced
1 cup olive oil
2 teaspoons dried cilantro
1 teaspoon cracked peppercorns
1 teaspoon garlic salt
1 (1½ pound) pork tenderloin
1-pound kale, stems removed and leaves coarsely chopped

1. Preheat an oven to 350°F. Mix lime juice and olive oil in a small bowl. Spice with peppercorns, garlic salt and cilantro. 2. Brush 3 tablespoons lime dressing on pork tenderloin. Wrap in aluminum foil; put into big baking dish. In preheated oven, roast till meat thermometer reads 170°F for 30-45 minutes. 3. As tenderloin cooks, put kale into steamer; cook till tender for 20 minutes. Slice pork tenderloin to 1½-inch thick slices; serve over kale. 4. Mix leftover dressing; drizzle on kale and pork.

Per Serving: Calories 518; Fat 37g; Sodium 563mg; Carbs 4g; Fiber 0g; Sugar 0g; Protein 36g

Grilled T-Bone Steaks

Prep time: 5 minutes | Cook time: 7 minutes | Serves: 2

4 teaspoons salt, or to taste
2 teaspoons paprika
1½ teaspoons ground black pepper
¾ teaspoon onion powder
¾ teaspoon garlic powder, or to taste
¾ teaspoon cayenne pepper, or to taste
¾ teaspoon ground coriander, or to taste
¾ teaspoon ground turmeric, or to taste
4 (16 ounce) T-bone steaks, at room temperature

1. Preheat outdoor grill to high heat and oil the grate lightly. In a small bowl, mix the turmeric, coriander, cayenne pepper, garlic powder, onion powder, black pepper, paprika and salt, then, set aside. 2. Using the spicing mixture, rub the steak on all sides. Cook for 3 to 3½ minutes per side for rare until desired doneness on the preheated grill. 3. The instant-read thermometer that was inserted in the middle should read 130°F.

Per Serving: Calories 538; Fat 44g; Sodium 952mg; Carbs 3g; Fiber 1g; Sugar 2g; Protein 31g

Pineapple Pork Roast

Prep time: 10 minutes | Cook time: 2 hours 30 minutes | Serves: 2

2 tablespoons olive oil
2 tablespoons chopped fresh rosemary, divided
1 teaspoon dried sage
1 (4 pound) bone-in pork shoulder roast, trimmed of excess fat
5 small garlic cloves, peeled and sliced
1 (14.4 ounce) can diced plum tomatoes
1 (15 ounce) can pineapple chunks, drained
1 large Vidalia onion, thinly sliced
Salt and pepper to taste

1. Turn the oven to 400°F to preheat. 2. In a big skillet, heat the olive oil over heat. Mix in sage and 1 tablespoon fresh rosemary. In the skillet, put the roast, and flip to brown all sides. Remove to a roasting pan. 3. Pierce a small knife into the top of the roast to make holes and insert with garlic slices. Pour over the roast with onion slices, pineapple and tomatoes. Sprinkle pepper, salt and the leftover rosemary over. 4. Put a cover on and cook for 30 minutes in the preheated oven. Lower the oven temperature to 300°F, and keep cooking until the internal temperature of the roast is at least 145°F, or about 2 hours.

Per Serving: Calories 493; Fat 40g; Sodium 857mg; Carbs 1g; Fiber 0g; Sugar 0g; Protein 31g

Pulled Pork with Barbeque Sauce

Prep time: 15 minutes | Cook time: 75 minutes | Serves: 2

1 (7 pound) pork shoulder roast, trimmed and cut into chunks
3 (12 fluid ounce) cans or bottles root beer
1 (18 ounce) bottle barbeque sauce

1. Put in the bottom of a pressure cooker the pork, then drizzle pork with root beer. Lock the lid onto pressure cooker and set over a burner on high heat. 2. Cook pork about 45 minutes. Follow manufacturer's instructions on how to release pressure from the cooker prior to checking the tenderness of meat. Meat should be soft enough to be pulled apart easily. If the pork is still not yet done enough, lock the lid on the cooker again and keep on cooking on high heat for 30 more minutes. 3. Release the pressure from cooker and drain liquid, then Place meat to a big bowl. Use 2 forks to pull pork into strands. 4. Drizzle pork with barbeque sauce and stir to coat well.

Per Serving: Calories 224; Fat 16g; Sodium 822mg; Carbs 0g; Fiber 0g; Sugar 0g; Protein 20g

Chapter 5 Fish and Seafood Recipes

62	Salmon Bake	67	Spicy Lemony Swordfish
62	Tasty Tiger Prawns and Bitter Melon	68	Tender Baked Haddock
63	Catfish and Veggie Gumbo	68	Grilled Salmon with Avocado Salsa
63	Cheesy Tuna Spread	69	Healthy Tuna Steaks with Noodles
64	Grilled Shrimp Skewers	69	Delicious Shrimp Sushi Rolls
64	Lemony Halibut	70	Traditional White Fish Curry
65	Salmon and Tomato Stew	70	Grilled Garlicky Oysters
65	Salmon Nori Rolls	71	Garlic Butter Lobster Tails
66	Delicious Garlic Shrimp	71	Cheesy Garlic Cod
66	Sea Bass with Juicy Broccoli	72	Cod and Cherry Tomatoes Platter
67	Baked Garlicky Snapper	72	Refreshing Shrimp Salad

Salmon Bake

Prep time: 5 minutes | Cook time: 20 minutes | Serves: 3

1-pound salmon fillet, halved
1 small tomato, chopped
5 green onions, chopped
¼ teaspoon salt
¼ teaspoon pepper

1. Start preheating the oven to 350°F. In the baking dish or a lightly greased sheet pan, put salmon; for even cooking, fold under the thin outer edges of the fillets. 2. Place green onions and chopped tomatoes on top of salmon. 3. Spice with pepper and salt. In prepared oven, cook salmon, uncovered, bake for about 20 minutes. When the fish is flaked easily with fork, it is done.

Per Serving: Calories 257; Fat 9g; Sodium 661mg; Carbs 23g; Fiber4 g; Sugar 4g; Protein 21g

Tasty Tiger Prawns and Bitter Melon

Prep time: 5 minutes | Cook time: 25 minutes | Serves: 2

2 tablespoons olive oil
1 small onion, diced
2 cloves garlic, crushed
½ pound pork loin, cut into small cubes
½ pound tiger prawns, peeled and deveined
1 tomato, chopped
salt and pepper to taste
1 bitter melon, seeded and sliced

1. In a skillet set on medium heat, add olive oil. Cook the garlic and onion in the hot oil for 5 minutes until scented. Stir the pork into the garlic and onion; cook for 5 minutes, until not pink. 2. Mix the prawns into the mixture then cook for 5 more minutes until not translucent. Mix in tomatoes; add pepper and salt to taste. 3. Keep on cooking for 5 minutes until the tomatoes soften. Mix the bitter melon through the mixture then cook for 5 minutes until the melon is tender. Serve immediately.

Per Serving: Calories 296; Fat 4g; Sodium 304mg; Carbs 62g; Fiber4 g; Sugar 40g; Protein 4g

Catfish and Veggie Gumbo

Prep time: 10 minutes | Cook time: 55 minutes | Serves: 2

1-pound catfish fillets, cut into 1 inch pieces
¼ cup vegetable oil
½ cup celery, chopped
½ cup green bell pepper, chopped
½ cup onion, chopped
1 clove garlic, chopped
2 cups water
2 cubes beef bouillon
2 (8 ounce) cans diced tomatoes
1 (10 ounce) package frozen okra
1 teaspoon salt
¼ teaspoon red pepper flakes
¼ teaspoon dried thyme
1 bay leaf
⅛ teaspoon hot pepper sauce

1. Pour 2 cups of water in a 3-quart pot, bring to a boil. Add bouillon cubes to boiling water and stir until fully dissolved. Heat vegetable oil in a skillet. Add garlic, onion, green pepper and celery and cook until softened. 2. Add cooked vegetables, okra and tomatoes to boiling water. Add hot pepper sauce, bay leaf, thyme, red pepper flakes and salt to season. 3. Lower the heat and simmer, covered for 30 minutes. Add catfish and simmer with a cover for 15 minutes or until catfish is softened and flaky.

Per Serving: Calories 257; Fat 9g; Sodium 661mg; Carbs 23g; Fiber4 g; Sugar 4g; Protein 21g

Cheesy Tuna Spread

Prep time: 5 minutes | Cook time: 0 minutes | Serves: 6

1 (6 ounce) can tuna in oil, drained
½ cup Ricotta cheese
½ teaspoon turmeric
2 ounces pecans, ground
1 tablespoon fresh cilantro, chopped

1. Blend tuna, Ricotta cheese, turmeric powder and pecans in a blender. Place to a serving bowl and serve garnished with fresh cilantro. 2. Serve with veggie sticks. Bon appétit!

Per Serving: Calories 257; Fat 9g; Sodium 661mg; Carbs 23g; Fiber4 g; Sugar 4g; Protein 21g

Grilled Shrimp Skewers

Prep time: 5 minutes | Cook time: 5 minutes | Serves: 2

¼ cup olive oil

¼ cup lemon juice

3 tablespoons chopped fresh parsley

1 tablespoon minced garlic

Ground black pepper to taste

Crushed red pepper flakes to taste (optional)

1½ pounds shrimp, peeled and deveined

1. Mix lemon juice, olive oil, black pepper, parsley and garlic in a nonreactive, big bowl. Put in some crushed red pepper for some spice but this is optional. Put in the shrimps and mix well to coat. Keep the marinade in the fridge for 30 minutes. 2. Set the grill on high heat and preheat. Insert the marinated shrimps onto the skewers bending each shrimp so that it is pierced once near the head and tail. Throw away the remaining marinade. 3. Lightly grease the grill grate. Put the shrimp skewers on the preheated grill and grill for 2 to 3 minutes per side or until the shrimp turns opaque.

Per Serving: Calories 255; Fat 14g; Sodium 676mg; Carbs 20g; Fiber 3g; Sugar 9g; Protein 11g

Lemony Halibut

Prep time: 10 minutes | Cook time: 20 minutes | Serves: 2

2 halibut fillets, boneless

A pinch of salt and black pepper

2 tablespoons ghee, melted

½ cup veggie stock

Juice of ½ lemon

2 tablespoons parsley, chopped

1. Heat up a pan with the ghee over -high heat, add halibut. Spice with salt and pepper, cook for 3 minutes on each side. Add the stock, lemon juice and parsley, cover the pan, reduce heat to medium and cook for 10 minutes more. 2. Divide the fish between plates, drizzle the cooking juices all over and serve. Enjoy!

Per Serving: Calories 296; Fat 4g; Sodium 304mg; Carbs 62g; Fiber4 g; Sugar 40g; Protein 4g

Salmon and Tomato Stew

Prep time: 5 minutes | Cook time: 20 minutes | Serves: 2

1 tablespoon olive oil
4 cloves garlic, minced
1 onion, diced
1 tomato, diced
1 (14.75 ounce) can pink salmon

2½ cups water
Bay leaf (optional)
Salt and ground black pepper to taste
1 teaspoon fish sauce (optional)

1. In a skillet set on medium heat, add olive oil. Mix in the onion and garlic; stir and cook for 5 minutes until the onion is tender and glassy. 2. Mix in tomato and cook until tender, then put in the salmon. Flake the salmon and keep on cooking for 3 minutes. 3. Mix in fish sauce, pepper, salt bay leaf, and water. Make it to a simmer. Cook for 20 minutes, covered.

Per Serving: Calories 296; Fat 4g; Sodium 304mg; Carbs 62g; Fiber4 g; Sugar 40g; Protein 4g

Salmon Nori Rolls

Prep time: 10 minutes | Cook time: 0 minutes | Serves: 3

3 nori sheets
5 ounce canned salmon, dried and flaked
1 red bell pepper, cut into thin strips
1 small avocado, pitted, peeled and cut into thin strips

1 small cucumber, cut into thin strips
1 spring onion, chopped
1 tablespoon mayonnaise
Coconut aminos for serving

1. Place the nori sheets on a cutting board, divide the salmon, bell pepper, avocado, cucumber, onion and mayonnaise, roll well, cut each roll in 2 pieces and serve with coconut aminos on the side. 2. Enjoy!

Per Serving: Calories 257; Fat 9g; Sodium 661mg; Carbs 23g; Fiber4 g; Sugar 4g; Protein 21g

Delicious Garlic Shrimp

Prep time: 10 minutes | Cook time: 50 minutes | Serves: 4

2 pounds shrimp, peeled and deveined
1 tablespoons parsley, chopped
A pinch of salt and black pepper
¼ teaspoon red pepper flakes, crushed
1 teaspoon smoked paprika
6 garlic cloves, minced
¾ cup olive oil

1. In slow cooker, mix oil, garlic, paprika, salt, pepper and red pepper flakes, stir, cover and cook on High for 30 minutes. 2. Add shrimp and parsley, cover and cook on High for 10 minutes more. 3. Stir again, cover pot again and cook on High for 10 minutes. Divide between plates and serve.

Per Serving: Calories 257; Fat 9g; Sodium 661mg; Carbs 23g; Fiber4 g; Sugar 4g; Protein 21g

Sea Bass with Juicy Broccoli

Prep time: 10 minutes | Cook time: 12 minutes | Serves: 2

2 sea bass fillets, boneless and skin scored
1 orange, peeled and cut into segments
1 broccoli head, florets separated
A pinch of salt and black pepper
3 tablespoons olive oil
4 tablespoons capers
Juice of 1 lemon

1. Heat up a pan with 2 tablespoons oil over -high heat, add fish fillets, spice with salt and pepper, cook for 4 minutes skin side down, flip, cook for 2 more minutes and divide between plates. 2. Heat up a pan with the rest of the oil over -high heat, add broccoli, orange segments, salt, pepper, capers and lemon juice, toss, cook for 6 minutes more, divide next to the fish and serve.

Per Serving: Calories 296; Fat 4g; Sodium 304mg; Carbs 62g; Fiber4 g; Sugar 40g; Protein 4g

Baked Garlicky Snapper

Prep time: 10 minutes | Cook time: 15 minutes | Serves: 2

2 red snapper fillets, boneless
Cooking spray
4 tablespoons ghee, melted
2 garlic cloves, minced
½ teaspoon Cajun seasoning
2 teaspoons parsley, chopped
A pinch of salt and black pepper
1 teaspoon chives, chopped
2 tablespoons parmesan, grated

1. Heat up a pan with the ghee over -high heat, add garlic, salt, pepper and Cajun seasoning, stir and cook for 3 minutes. Spray a baking dish with the cooking spray and place the fish fillets inside. 2. Brush them with the ghee and garlic mix, sprinkle parsley, chives and parmesan, Put in the oven and bake for 12 minutes at 400°F. 3. Divide the fish between plates and serve with a side salad.

Per Serving: Calories 257; Fat 9g; Sodium 661mg; Carbs 23g; Fiber4 g; Sugar 4g; Protein 21g

Spicy Lemony Swordfish

Prep time: 10 minutes | Cook time: 20 minutes | Serves: 6

6 swordfish steaks
½ cup olive oil
A pinch of salt and black pepper
¼ cup lemon juice
A dash of hot sauce
¼ teaspoon sweet paprika

1. In a bowl, Add and mix the oil with salt, pepper, hot sauce and paprika and Mix well. Brush the fish steaks with this mixture, place them in a baking dish, drizzle the lemon juice all over. 2. Put in the oven and bake at 350°F for 20 minutes. Divide the fish between plates and serve. 3. Enjoy!

Per Serving: Calories 296; Fat 4g; Sodium 304mg; Carbs 62g; Fiber4 g; Sugar 40g; Protein 4g

Tender Baked Haddock

Prep time: 10 minutes | Cook time: 30 minutes | Serves: 4

1-pound haddock
3 teaspoons water
2 tablespoons lemon juice
Salt and ground black pepper, to taste
2 tablespoons mayonnaise
1 teaspoon dill weed
Vegetable oil cooking spray
A pinch of Old Bay seasoning

1. Spray a baking dish with some cooking oil. Add lemon juice, water, fish, and toss to coat. Add salt, pepper, Old Bay seasoning, dill, and toss again. 2. Add mayonnaise and spread well. Place in an oven at 350ºF and bake for 30 minutes. Divide on plates and serve.

Per Serving: Calories 257; Fat 9g; Sodium 661mg; Carbs 23g; Fiber4 g; Sugar 4g; Protein 21g

Grilled Salmon with Avocado Salsa

Prep time: 10 minutes | Cook time: 8 minutes | Serves: 4

4 salmon fillets
1 teaspoon cumin; ground
1 teaspoon sweet paprika
½ teaspoon ancho chili powder
For the salsa:
1 small red onion; chopped.
1 avocado; pitted, peeled and chopped.
2 tablespoons cilantro; chopped.
1 teaspoon onion powder
1 tablespoon olive oil
Salt and black pepper to the taste.

Juice from 2 limes
Salt and black pepper to the taste.

1. In a bowl, mix salt, pepper, chili powder, onion powder, paprika and cumin. Rub salmon with this mixture, drizzle the oil and rub again and cook on preheated grill for 4 minutes on each side. 2. Meanwhile; in a bowl, mix avocado with red onion, salt, pepper, cilantro and lime juice and stir. 3. Divide salmon between plates and top each fillet with avocado salsa.

Per Serving: Calories 296; Fat 4g; Sodium 304mg; Carbs 62g; Fiber4 g; Sugar 40g; Protein 4g

Healthy Tuna Steaks with Noodles

Prep time: 5 minutes | Cook time: 25 minutes | Serves: 4

1 pack (7 oz.) miracle noodle angel hair
3 cups water
Cooking spray
1 red bell pepper, seeded and halved
4 tuna steaks
Salt and black pepper to taste
Olive oil for brushing
2 tablespoons pickled ginger
2 tablespoons chopped cilantro

1. In a colander, rinse the noodles with running cold water. Bring a pot of salted water to a boil; blanch the noodles for 2 minutes. Drain and Place to a dry skillet over medium heat. Dry roast for a minute until opaque. 2. Grease a grill's grate with cooking spray and preheat the grill to medium heat. Season the red bell pepper and tuna with salt and black pepper, brush with olive oil, and grill covered. Cook both for 3 minutes on each side. Place to a plate to cool. Dice bell pepper with a knife. 3. Assemble the noodles, tuna, and bell pepper in serving plate. Top with pickled ginger and garnish with cilantro. 4. Serve with roasted sesame sauce.

Per Serving: Calories 255; Fat 14g; Sodium 676mg; Carbs 20g; Fiber 3g; Sugar 9g; Protein 11g

Delicious Shrimp Sushi Rolls

Prep time: 5 minutes | Cook time: 10 minutes | Serves: 5

2 cups cooked and chopped shrimp
1 tablespoon sriracha sauce
¼ cucumber, julienned
5 hand roll nori sheets
¼ cup mayonnaise

1. Add and mix shrimp, mayonnaise, and sriracha in a bowl. Lay out a single nori sheet on a flat surface and spread about ⅕ of the shrimp mixture and cucumber. 2. Roll the nori sheet as desired. 3. Repeat with the other ingredients.

Per Serving: Calories 296; Fat 4g; Sodium 304mg; Carbs 62g; Fiber 4 g; Sugar 40g; Protein 4g

Traditional White Fish Curry

Prep time: 5 minutes | Cook time: 35 minutes | Serves: 4

4 white fish fillets
½ teaspoon mustard seeds
1-inch turmeric root; grated
¼ cup cilantro
1½ cups coconut cream
3 garlic cloves; minced
2 green chilies; chopped.

1 teaspoon ginger; grated
1 teaspoon curry powder
¼ teaspoon cumin; ground
4 tablespoons coconut oil
1 small red onion; chopped.
Salt and black pepper to the taste.

1. Heat up a pot with half of the coconut oil over heat; add mustard seeds and cook for 2 minutes. Add ginger, onion and garlic; stir and cook for 5 minutes. Add turmeric, curry powder, chilies and cumin; stir and cook for 5 minutes more. 2. Add coconut milk, salt and pepper; stir, bring to a boil and cook for 15 minutes. Heat up a pan with the rest of the oil over medium heat; add fish; stir and cook for 3 minutes. 3. Add this to the curry sauce; stir and cook for 5 minutes more. Add cilantro; stir, divide into bowls and serve.

Per Serving: Calories 257; Fat 9g; Sodium 661mg; Carbs 23g; Fiber4 g; Sugar 4g; Protein 21g

Grilled Garlicky Oysters

Prep time: 5 minutes | Cook time: 8 minutes | Serves: 3

6 big oysters, shucked
3 garlic cloves, minced
A pinch of sweet paprika

2 tablespoons melted ghee
1 lemon cut in wedges
1 tablespoon parsley

1. Top each oyster with melted ghee, parsley, paprika and ghee. 2. Place them on preheated grill over medium high heat and cook for 8 minutes. 3. Serve them with lemon wedges on the side

Per Serving: Calories 296; Fat 4g; Sodium 304mg; Carbs 62g; Fiber4 g; Sugar 40g; Protein 4g

Garlic Butter Lobster Tails

Prep time: 5 minutes | Cook time: 15 minutes | Serves: 4

10 tablespoons butter

4 lobster tails, top removed and deveined

½ cup garlic, minced

Sea salt, smoked paprika and white pepper

1. Preheat the broiler to high heat and grease a baking sheet. Heat 4 tablespoons butter in a skillet and add garlic. Sauté for about 2 minutes and set aside. 2. Mix sea salt, smoked paprika and white pepper in a bowl. 3. Place the lobster tails on the baking sheet and sprinkle with the spice mixture. Drizzle with half the garlic butter and Place to the oven. 4. Bake for about 10 minutes, drizzling rest of the garlic butter in between. 5. Remove from the oven and serve warm.

Per Serving: Calories 257; Fat 9g; Sodium 661mg; Carbs 23g; Fiber4 g; Sugar 4g; Protein 21g

Cheesy Garlic Cod

Prep time: 1 hour | Cook time: 20 minutes | Serves: 6

1 tablespoon extra-virgin olive oil

1 (2½pound) cod fillet

¼ cup parmesan cheese, finely grated

Salt and black pepper, to taste

5 garlic cloves, minced

1. Preheat the oven to 400°F and grease a baking dish with cooking spray. Mix the olive oil, garlic, parmesan cheese, salt and black pepper in a bowl. Marinate the cod fillets in this mixture for about 1 hour. Place to the baking dish and cover with foil. 2. Put in the oven and bake for about 20 minutes. Remove from the oven and serve warm.

Per Serving: Calories 255; Fat 14g; Sodium 676mg; Carbs 20g; Fiber 3g; Sugar 9g; Protein 11g

Cod and Cherry Tomatoes Platter

Prep time: 10 minutes | Cook time: 30 minutes | Serves: 6

1-pound cherry tomatoes, halved
6 (4 ounce) cod fillets
3 garlic cloves, minced
Salt and black pepper, to taste
2 tablespoons olive oil

1. Preheat the oven to 375°F and grease a baking dish. Put half the cherry tomatoes in the baking dish and layer with cod fillets. Spice with garlic, salt and black pepper and drizzle with olive oil. 2. Place remaining tomatoes on the cod fillets and Place to the oven. Bake for about 30 minutes and dish out to serve hot.

Per Serving: Calories 296; Fat 4g; Sodium 304mg; Carbs 62g; Fiber4 g; Sugar 40g; Protein 4g

Refreshing Shrimp Salad

Prep time: 10 minutes | Cook time: 10 minutes | Serves: 4

1-pound shrimp; peeled and deveined
2 tablespoons olive oil
2 tablespoons lime juice
2 tablespoons mayonnaise
1 teaspoon lime zest
½ cup sour cream
3 endives; leaves separated
3 tablespoons parsley; chopped.
2 teaspoons mint; chopped.
1 tablespoon tarragon; chopped.
1 tablespoon lemon juice
Salt and black pepper to the taste.

1. In a bowl, mix shrimp with salt, pepper and the olive oil, toss to coat and spread them on a lined baking sheet. 2. Place shrimp in the oven at 400°F and bake for 10 minutes Add lime juice, toss them to coat again and leave aside. 3. In a bowl, mix mayo with sour cream, lime zest, lemon juice, salt, pepper, tarragon, mint and parsley and stir very well. 4. Chop shrimp, add to salad dressing, toss to coat everything and spoon into endive leaves. 5. Serve right away.

Per Serving: Calories 257; Fat 9g; Sodium 661mg; Carbs 23g; Fiber4 g; Sugar 4g; Protein 21g

Chapter 6 Snack and Appetizer Recipes

74	Roasted Potatoes	80	Herbed Button Mushrooms
74	Antioxidant Nuts Mix	80	Garlicky Bell Pepper and Tomato
75	Pineapple Salad with Avocado	81	Carrots and Tomatoes Salad
75	Spiced Turkey Wings	81	Sweet Potato Sticks
76	Crispy Squash Fries	82	Cheesy Sausage Dip
76	Simple Paprika Potato Slices	82	Almond Crusted Zucchini Slices
77	Cajun French Fries	83	Bacon Chicken Skewers
77	"Hummus" of Spinach and Carrot	83	Tasty Goat Skewers
78	Delicious Chili Hash Browns	84	Cheesy Tomatoes with Basil Dressing
78	Marinated Spiced Eggs	85	Savory Sweet Potatoes
79	Nutty Carrots	86	Tortilla Chips
79	Caprese Eggplant Roll Ups		

Roasted Potatoes

Prep time: 15 minutes | Cook time: 55 minutes | Serves: 2

2 pounds new yellow potatoes, halved
3 sprigs fresh rosemary
3 cloves garlic, whole, peeled, bruised
2 bay leaves
2 tablespoons salt
2 tablespoons olive oil
1 pinch cayenne pepper
1 pinch kosher salt

1. Put potatoes in a big pot of water. Bruise rosemary with the blunt side of a knife blade; put in pot. Add salt, bay leaves and garlic; boil then simmer for 5 minutes, drain; air fry potatoes. Preheat an oven to 375°F. 2. Put back into pot when potatoes are thoroughly dry. Drizzle pinch of salt, cayenne pepper and olive oil over; mix to coat. 3. Put potatoes onto rimmed sheet pan; bake for 35-45 minutes, varying from potato's size, till flesh is soft and creamy and potatoes are crusty and golden brown.

Per Serving: Calories 150; Total Fat 6g; Saturated Fat 0.9g; Sodium 150mg; Carbs 10g; Fiber 3g; Sugar 2g; Protein 14g

Antioxidant Nuts Mix

Prep time: 5 minutes | Cook time: 0 minutes | Serves: 2

¼ cup almonds
¼ cup walnuts
¼ cup pumpkin seeds
¼ cup sunflower seeds
¼ cup dried cranberries
¼ cup goji berries
¼ cup raisins
¼ cup semisweet chocolate chips (optional)

1. Mix chocolate chips, raisins, goji berries, cranberries, sunflower seeds, pumpkin seeds, walnuts and almonds in bowl.

Per Serving: Calories 100; Total Fat 6g; Saturated Fat 0.9g; Sodium 50mg; Carbs 1g; Fiber 0g; Sugar 0g; Protein 10g

Pineapple Salad with Avocado

Prep time: 5 minutes | Cook time: 0 minutes | Serves: 2

- 1½ cups cucumbers peeled, seeded, and cubed
- ½ cup chopped red onion
- 2 tablespoons chopped serrano pepper
- 2 tablespoons lime juice
- ¾ teaspoon salt
- 2½ cups pineapple, peeled and cut into ½ inch dice
- 2 avocado peeled, pitted and diced

1. In a large bowl, Add and mix salt, lime juice, serrano pepper, onion and cucumbers. 2. Add avocado and pineapple. Toss gently till combined.

Per Serving: Calories 90; Total Fat 1.5g; Saturated Fat 0.4g; Sodium 180mg; Carbs 14g; Fiber 3g; Sugar 1g; Protein 6g

Spiced Turkey Wings

Prep time: 5 minutes | Cook time: 2-3 hours | Serves: 2

- 8 turkey wings, tips discarded
- 2 tablespoons salt-free seasoning blend
- 2 teaspoons paprika
- 1 teaspoon celery salt
- Salt and ground black pepper to taste
- 1 large onion, coarsely chopped
- 4 cloves garlic, coarsely chopped

1. Preheat the oven to 250°F. Pat dry turkey wings using paper towels. Cut to 3-4 pieces. In a small bowl, mix pepper, salt, celery salt, paprika and seasoning blend. 2. Lightly coat wing pieces with seasoning mixture. 3. In a 9x13in baking dish, put wing pieces. Spread garlic and onion on wings. Use aluminum foil to cover. 4. In the middle of the preheated oven, put baking dish. Bake for about 2½ hours until wings are pierced easily with a fork. 5. Put oven temperature to 350°F. Discard aluminum foil. Bake for 15-20 more minutes until wings are browned well.

Per Serving: Calories 90; Total Fat 2.5g; Saturated Fat 0.3g; Sodium 75mg; Carbs 3g; Fiber 0g; Sugar 1g; Protein 16g

Crispy Squash Fries

Prep time: 5 minutes | Cook time: 20 minutes | Serves: 2

1 (2 pound) butternut squash, halved and seeded

Pinch of salt, to taste

1. Preheat the oven to 425°F. Cut away the peel from the squash with a sharp knife. Slice the squash into sticks resembles French fries. 2. On a baking sheet, lay squash pieces and spice with salt. 3. Bake for 20 minutes in the preheated oven, halfway through baking, flip the fries over. Once fries start to brown on the edges and become crispy, fries are done.

Per Serving: Calories 100; Total Fat 6g; Saturated Fat 0.9g; Sodium 95mg; Carbs 8g; Fiber 2g; Sugar 2g; Protein 5g

Simple Paprika Potato Slices

Prep time: 10 minutes | Cook time: 4 minutes | Serves: 4

4 potatoes, peeled and sliced
½ teaspoon smoked paprika
Salt and pepper, to taste

1 tablespoon coconut oil
Water, as needed

1. Place the potato slices inside the Instant Pot and pour enough water to just cover them. Close the lid and turn clockwise to seal. Select "MANUAL" and set the cooking time to 2 minutes. Cook on HIGH pressure. 2. When the timer goes off, press the "KEEP WARM/CANCEL" button. Turn the pressure handle to "Venting" to release the pressure quickly and then open the lid carefully. Drain the potatoes and discard the water. Place the potatoes to a bowl. Wipe the Instant Pot clean. 3. Select the "SAUTE" mode and add the coconut oil to it. Sprinkle the potatoes with paprika, salt, and pepper, and toss to mix well, but be careful not to break them. 4. When the oil is melted, add the potato slices to the pot and cook for about a minute per side. Serve and enjoy!

Per Serving: Calories 76; Total Fat 7g; Saturated Fat 1g; Sodium 82mg; Carbs 4g; Fiber 3g; Sugar 0g; Protein 1g

Cajun French Fries

Prep time: 5 minutes | Cook time: 45 minutes | Serves: 2

¼ cup olive oil

1 teaspoon garlic powder

1 teaspoon onion powder

1 teaspoon chili powder

1 teaspoon Cajun seasoning

1 teaspoon sea salt

6 large baking potatoes, sliced into thin wedges

1. Preheat oven to 400°F. In a large resealable bag, mix sea salt, Cajun seasoning, chili powder, onion powder, garlic powder, and olive oil. 2. Add potatoes. Toss to coat the potatoes evenly with the seasoned oil. 3. Spread potatoes in a single layer on a baking sheet. Bake in the oven for 35 minutes. 4. Use a spatula to stir the potatoes and continue cooking for about 10 more minutes until crispy.

Per Serving: Calories 100; Total Fat 28g; Saturated Fat 1.2g; Sodium 150mg; Carbs 8g; Fiber 4g; Sugar 2g; Protein 2g

"Hummus" of Spinach and Carrot

Prep time: 10 minutes | Cook time: 5 minutes | Serves: 6

3 cups chopped carrots

3 tablespoons tahini

2 cups chopped spinach

1 garlic clove, crushed

2 tablespoons lemon juice

2 tablespoons olive oil

2 cups water

Salt and pepper, to taste

1. Add and mix the carrots and water in Instant Pot. Close the lid and turn clockwise to seal. Select the "MANUAL" cooking mode. Set the cooking time to 4 minutes. Cook on HIGH pressure. 2. When the timer goes off, move the handle to "Venting" to release the pressure quickly. Open the lid and drain the carrots. Place them to a food processor. Add the remaining ingredients and process until the mixture becomes smooth.

Per Serving: Calories 240; Total Fat 6g; Saturated Fat 1.5g; Sodium 280mg; Carbs 0g; Fiber 0g; Sugar 0g; Protein 42g

Delicious Chili Hash Browns

Prep time: 10 minutes | Cook time: 10 minutes | Serves: 4

1 pound potatoes, peeled and grated
1 teaspoon chili powder
¼ teaspoon smoked paprika
¼ teaspoon black pepper
½ teaspoon sea salt
1½ tablespoons coconut oil

1. Turn the Instant Pot on and set it to "SAUTE". Add the coconut oil to the pot. When the oil becomes melted, add the potatoes. Combine well with the spices. 2. Press them with a spatula and cook for about 5 minutes. Flip the potatoes over and cook for 5 minutes. 3. Divide the chili hash browns between 4 plates. Enjoy!

Per Serving: Calories 100; Total Fat 3.5g; Saturated Fat 1.5g; Sodium 210mg; Carbs 9g; Fiber 2g; Sugar 2g; Protein 8g

Marinated Spiced Eggs

Prep time: 10 minutes | Cook time: 7 minutes | Serves: 4

6 eggs
1¼ cups water
¼ cup unsweetened rice vinegar
2 tablespoons coconut aminos
Salt and ground black pepper, to taste
2 garlic cloves, peeled and minced
1 teaspoon stevia
4 ounces cream cheese
1 tablespoon fresh chives, chopped

1. Put eggs in a pot, add water to cover, bring to a boil over medium heat, cover, and cook for 7 minutes. 2. Rinse eggs with cold water, and set them aside to cool down. In a bowl, mix 1 cup water with coconut aminos, vinegar, stevia, and garlic. 3. Put eggs in this mixture, cover with kitchen towel, and set aside for 2 hours, rotating them from time to time. 4. Peel eggs, cut in half, and put the egg yolks in a bowl. 5. Add remaining water, cream cheese, salt, pepper, chives, and stir well. Stuff egg whites with mixture and serve.

Per Serving: Calories 410; Total Fat 12g; Saturated Fat 1g; Sodium 570mg; Carbs 53g; Fiber 7g; Sugar 8g; Protein 29g

Nutty Carrots

Prep time: 10 minutes | Cook time: 5 minutes | Serves: 8

¼ cup olive oil
3½ cups water
3 pounds carrots, peeled and cut into matchsticks
¼ cup chopped nuts by choice (walnuts and pine nuts are great)
2 tablespoons balsamic vinegar
1 tablespoon orange juice
2 teaspoons lemon juice
½ teaspoon onion powder

1. Add and mix the water and carrots in Instant Pot. Close the lid and turn clockwise to seal. Select the "MANUAL" cooking mode. Set the cooking time to 5 minutes and cook on HIGH. 2. When the timer goes off, press the "KEEP WARM/CANCEL" button. Turn the pressure handle to "Venting" for a quick pressure release and open the lid carefully. 3. Drain the carrots and place in a bowl. Mix the vinegar, orange juice, lemon juice, onion powder, and olive oil. Pour the mixture over the carrots and toss to coat well. Sprinkle the nuts over. 4. Serve and enjoy!

Per Serving: Calories 61; Total Fat 5g; Saturated Fat 1g; Sodium 151mg; Carbs 1g; Fiber 0g; Sugar 1g; Protein 3g

Caprese Eggplant Roll Ups

Prep time: 10 minutes | Cook time: 7 minutes | Serves: 2

2 oz. mozzarella cheese, thinly sliced
½ eggplant, thinly sliced
½ large tomato, thinly sliced
3 tablespoons olive oil
1 basil leaf, thinly shredded
¼ teaspoon black pepper

1. Brush the eggplant slices with olive oil and keep aside. Heat a griddle pan and place the eggplant slices in a pan. 2. Grill for about 3 minutes on each side and top with mozzarella slice, tomato slice, basil leaf and black pepper. Grill for 1 minute and roll the eggplant holding it with a cocktail stick. 3. Dish out and serve warm.

Per Serving: Calories 290; Total Fat 11g; Saturated Fat 2g; Sodium 370mg; Carbs 14g; Fiber 5g; Sugar 7g; Protein 33g

Herbed Button Mushrooms

Prep time: 5 minutes | Cook time: 4 minutes | Serves: 6

1½ lbs. fresh button mushrooms, rinsed
1 cup white wine
2 tablespoons of vinegar
½ cup olive oil
½ teaspoon garlic powder

Salt and freshly ground pepper to taste
1 dash hot pepper powder
1 pinch parsley flakes
1 pinch of dry basil

1. In a large pot, place all ingredients and cook for 3-4 minutes on -high heat. Remove from the heat, and allow to cool. 2. Place mushrooms in colander to drain. Serve or keep refrigerated.

Per Serving: Calories 320; Total Fat 15g; Saturated Fat 2.5g; Sodium 410mg; Carbs 10g; Fiber 4g; Sugar 5g; Protein 36g

Garlicky Bell Pepper and Tomato

Prep time: 5 minutes | Cook time: 10 minutes | Serves: 46

1 pounds bell peppers, cut into strips
2 large tomatoes, chopped
1 cup tomato sauce
¼ cup chicken broth

1 tablespoon minced garlic
2 tablespoon chopped parsley
1 tablespoon olive oil
Salt and pepper

1. Turn the Instant Pot on and set it to "SAUTE". Add the olive oil to it. When hot and sizzling, add the peppers and cook for 2-3 minutes. 2. Add garlic and sauté for 1 minute. Stir in the remaining ingredients. Close the lid and turn clockwise to seal. Select the "MANUAL" cooking mode. 3. Set the cooking time to 6 minutes. Cook on HIGH pressure. After the beeping sound, press the "KEEP WARM/CANCEL" button. 4. Turn the pressure handle to "Venting" to do a quick pressure release. Open the lid gently. Serve and enjoy!

Per Serving: Calories 40; Total Fat 2.5g; Saturated Fat 1.2g; Sodium 100mg; Carbs 1g; Fiber 0g; Sugar 1g; Protein 3g

Carrots and Tomatoes Salad

Prep time: 60 minutes | Cook time: 8 minutes | Serves: 6

1 cup chopped onions

1 cup chopped carrots

2 cups chopped tomatoes

½ cup chopped bell peppers

2 tablespoons chopped cilantro

1 teaspoon minced garlic

¼ cup lime juice

1 jalapeno, deseed and minced

1 tablespoon olive oil

½ teaspoon sea salt

¼ teaspoon pepper

1. Turn the Instant Pot on and set it to "SAUTE". Add the olive oil and heat until sizzling. Add the onions, peppers, and carrots, and cook for 4 minutes. Add tomatoes and cook for 3 more minutes. Stir in the garlic and sauté just for 1 minute. Place the mixture to a bowl and let cool for about 15 minutes. 2. Stir in the remaining ingredients. Cover the bowl with a plastic wrap and place it in the fridge. 3. Let sit in the fridge for about 45 minutes before serving. Enjoy!

Per Serving: Calories 100; Total Fat 8g; Saturated Fat 1.2g; Sodium 150mg; Carbs 8g; Fiber 4g; Sugar 2g;

Sweet Potato Sticks

Prep time: 5 minutes | Cook time: 40 minutes | Serves: 2

1 tablespoon olive oil

½ teaspoon paprika

8 sweet potatoes, sliced lengthwise into quarters

1. Heat the oven to 400°F. Grease lightly a cookie sheet. 2. In a big bowl, add and mix paprika and olive oil. Put the potato sticks in and mix by hand to coat. 3. Place on prepared baking sheet. Bake for 40 minutes in the oven.

Per Serving: Calories 110; Total Fat 3.5g; Saturated Fat 0.8g; Sodium 110mg; Carbs 2g; Fiber 0g; Sugar 1g; Protein 16g

Cheesy Sausage Dip

Prep time: 10 minutes | Cook time: 2 hours 15 minutes | Serves: 28

8 ounces cream cheese

A pinch of salt, and black pepper

16 ounces sour cream

8 ounces pepper jack cheese, chopped

15 ounces canned tomatoes mixed with habaneros

1 pound Italian sausage, ground

¼ cup green onions, chopped

1. Heat a pan over medium heat, add sausage, stir, and cook until it browns. 2. Add tomato mixture, stir, and cook for 4 minutes. 3. Add a pinch of salt and pepper and the green onions, stir, and cook for 4 minutes. 4. Spread pepper jack cheese on the bottom of a slow cooker. Add the cream cheese, sausage mixture, and sour cream, cover, and cook on high for 2 hours. 5. Uncover slow cooker, stir the dip, place to a bowl, and serve.

Per Serving: Calories 290; Total Fat 8g; Saturated Fat 1.5g; Sodium 480mg; Carbs 31g; Fiber 7g; Sugar 14g; Protein 24g

Almond Crusted Zucchini Slices

Prep time: 15 minutes | Cook time: 15 minutes | Serves: 6

2 large zucchinis, sliced into rings

1 cup almond flour

1 egg from free range chickens

Sea salt and ground black pepper to taste

1 teaspoon garlic powder

1 teaspoon onion powder

1 teaspoon fresh thyme

1. Preheat oven to 450°F. Line the baking sheet with a parchment paper and set aside. 2. In a bowl, beat the egg. In a separate bowl, Add and mix almond flour, salt and black pepper, garlic and onion powder, thyme. 3. Dip zucchini slices in the egg and let excess drip off, drop in the almond flour mixture to coat. Place coated zucchini slices onto prepared baking sheet. Bake for 13-15 minutes flipping once. 4. Serve warm.

Per Serving: Calories 550; Total Fat 26g; Saturated Fat 4g; Sodium 480mg; Carbs 35g; Fiber 10g; Sugar 6g; Protein 41g

Bacon Chicken Skewers

Prep time: 15 minutes | Cook time: 25 minutes | Serves: 6

2 chicken breast fillets, cut into cubes
Salt and ground pepper
10 slices of bacon
1 cup of cream cheese
1 cup of yogurt
2 tablespoons of mayonnaise
2 tablespoons of mustard

1. Cut the chicken into small pieces; season with salt and pepper. 2. In a bowl, mix mayonnaise, yogurt, mustard, and the salt and pepper. Add the chicken pieces and stir. Cover and refrigerate for 2 -3 hours. 3. Preheat the oven to 360°F. Cut bacon into bits. Thread chicken and bacon on skewers one after another. 4. Place the chicken-bacon skewers in a baking dish. Bake for 15 minutes, and then, turn over and bake for further 10 minutes. Serve hot.

Per Serving: Calories 480; Total Fat 18g; Saturated Fat 2.5g; Sodium 390mg; Carbs 54g; Fiber 6g; Sugar 13g; Protein 30g

Tasty Goat Skewers

Prep time: 20 minutes | Cook time: 10 minutes | Serves: 4

1 lb. boneless goat loin, cut into ½" cubes
Marinade:
1 tablespoon lemon juice
1 cup yogurt
¼ teaspoon ground ginger
½ teaspoon turmeric
½ teaspoon ground cumin
1 tablespoon ground coriander
½ teaspoon salt

1. Cut boneless goat loin into ½" cubes. 2. In a bowl, mix all ingredients for marinade. Add the goat to the bowl and stir to coat with the marinade evenly. Cover and refrigerate overnight. 3. Remove the bowl with marinated goat 15-20 minutes before grilling. 4. Preheat grill. Remove the meat from the marinade, and dry on kitchen paper towel. 5. Thread goat meat on skewers. Grill for about 4-5 minutes on each side. Serve hot.

Per Serving: Calories 290; Total Fat 11g; Saturated Fat 2g; Sodium 370mg; Carbs 14g; Fiber 5g; Sugar 7g; Protein 33g

Cheesy Tomatoes with Basil Dressing

Prep time: 10 minutes | Cook time: 25 minutes | Serves: 2

1 tablespoon olive oil

4 large ripe tomatoes, halved

2 tablespoons Balsamic vinegar

For the Dressing:

1 garlic clove

Small handful fresh basil

½ teaspoon lemon

Salt and black pepper, to taste

4 basil leaves

4 thin Mozzarella slices

Salt, to taste

2 tablespoons olive oil

1. Preheat the oven to 360°F and grease a baking sheet. Place the tomatoes on the baking sheet, cut side up. Drizzle the olive oil and Balsamic vinegar and spice with salt and black pepper. 2. Roast for about 20 minutes and top the tomatoes with the mozzarella cheese. Roast for 5 minutes and remove from the oven. Place a basil leaf on each bottom half and close with the top half. 3. For the dressing: Put all the ingredients in a small food processor until finely chopped. 4. Serve the tomatoes with the dressing.

Per Serving: Calories 360; Total Fat 18g; Saturated Fat 3g; Sodium 390mg; Carbs 15g; Fiber 4g; Sugar 7g; Protein 34g

Savory Sweet Potatoes

Prep time: 10 minutes | Cook time: 11 minutes | Serves: 6

2 pounds sweet potatoes

1 teaspoon sea salt

1 teaspoon pepper

2 tablespoons olive oil

1½ cups water

1. Pour the water into the Instant Pot and lower the trivet. Wash and peel the potatoes and place each of them on a piece of aluminum foil. Sprinkle the potatoes with salt and pepper and drizzle with olive oil. 2. Wrap them in foil and place the potato wraps on top of the trivet. Close the lid and turn clockwise to seal. Select the "MANUAL" cooking mode and set the time to 11 minutes. Make sure that you cook on HIGH pressure. 3. After the beep, press the "KEEP WARM/CANCEL" button. Turn the pressure handle to "Venting" for a quick pressure release. 4. Open the lid carefully and place the potatoes on the kitchen counter. Unwrap them gently, making sure that you keep hands away from the steam. Chop or slice them to your liking. 5. Enjoy!

Per Serving: Calories 280; Total Fat 12g; Saturated Fat 2g; Sodium 240mg; Carbs 3g; Fiber 1g; Sugar 2g; Protein 39g

Tortilla Chips

Prep time: 10 minutes | Cook time: 14 minutes | Serves: 6

For the Tortillas:

2 teaspoons olive oil

1 cup flaxseed meal

2 tablespoons psyllium husk powder

¼ teaspoon xanthan gum

1 cup water

½ teaspoon curry powder

3 teaspoons coconut flour

For the Chips:

6 flaxseed tortillas

Salt and ground black pepper, to taste

3 tablespoons vegetable oil

Fresh tomato paste, for serving

Sour cream, for serving

1. In a bowl, mix flaxseed meal with psyllium powder, olive oil, xanthan gum, water, curry powder, and mix until you obtain an elastic dough. Spread coconut flour on a working surface. 2. Divide dough into 6 pieces, place each piece on the work surface, roll into a circle, and cut each into 6 pieces. 3. Heat a pan with the vegetable oil over high heat, add the tortilla chips, cook for 2 minutes on each side, and Place to paper towels. 4. Put tortilla chips in a bowl, spice with salt, pepper, and serve with some fresh tomato paste, and sour cream on the side.

Per Serving: Calories 330; Total Fat 10g; Saturated Fat 2g; Sodium 420mg; Carbs 12g; Fiber 2g; Sugar 5g; Protein 31g

Chapter 7 Dessert Recipes

- 88 Bacon and Veggie Omelet Cupcakes
- 88 Almond and Coconut Apple Dessert
- 89 Easy Pear Wedges
- 89 Aromatic Lemony Apples
- 90 Chocolate Almond Banana Squares
- 90 Tropical Coconut and Pear Delight
- 91 Currant Poached Peaches
- 91 Delicious Apple and Peach Compote
- 92 Cinnamon Strawberry Cream
- 92 Traditional Berry Pie
- 93 Figs & Pecans Stuffed Apples
- 93 Dark Chocolate Cake
- 94 Lemon and berries Cream
- 94 Nutty Carrot Cake
- 95 Berries Cream
- 95 Energy Booster Bars
- 96 Stewed Figs and Pine Nuts
- 96 Silky Strawberry Marmalade
- 96 Simple Raspberry Cream
- 97 Almond Pomegranate Fudge
- 97 Cashew Apple Stew
- 98 Nuts and Berries Jelly

Bacon and Veggie Omelet Cupcakes

Prep time: 5 minutes | Cook time: 25 minutes | Serves: 4

4 bacon slices; chopped
A handful spinach; chopped
1 white onion; chopped
1 red bell pepper; chopped
1 green bell pepper; chopped
1 yellow bell pepper; chopped
1 tomato; chopped
8 eggs
A pinch of sea salt
Black pepper to the taste

1. Heat up a pan over medium high heat, add bacon, stir; cook until it's crispy, place to paper towels, drain grease and leave aside. Heat up the pan with the bacon fat over medium high heat, add onion, stir and cook for 3 minutes. 2. Add tomato, all bell peppers, a pinch of salt and black pepper, stir; cook for a couple more minutes and take off heat. 3. In a bowl, mix eggs with a pinch of salt and black pepper and mix with veggies and bacon. Stir, divide this into a lined muffin tray, put in the oven at 350°F and bake for 17 minutes. 4. Leave you special muffins to cool down, divide between plates and serve.

Per Serving: Calories 103; Fat 7g; Sodium 59mg; Carbs 13g; Fiber 2g; Sugar 1g; Protein 8g

Almond and Coconut Apple Dessert

Prep time: 10 minutes | Cook time: 4 minutes | Serves: 4

3 apples, peeled and diced
½ cup chopped or slivered almonds
½ cup coconut milk
¼ teaspoon cinnamon

1. Place all of the ingredients inside the Instant Pot. Stir well and put the lid on. Turn the lid clockwise to seal and press the "MANUAL" button. Set the cooking time to 4 minutes. Cook on HIGH pressure. 2. When the timer goes off, press the "KEEP WARM/CANCEL" button. Moe the handle from "Sealing" to "Venting" to release the pressure quickly. 3. Open the lid gently and divide the mixture between 4 serving bowls. Enjoy!

Per Serving: Calories 170; Fat 4g; Sodium 84mg; Carbs 15g; Fiber 4g; Sugar 1g; Protein 4g

Easy Pear Wedges

Prep time: 8 minutes | Cook time: 7 minutes | Serves: 3

2 large pears, peeled and cut into wedges
3 tablespoons almond butter
2 tablespoons coconut oil

1. Pour 1 cup of water into the Instant Pot. Place the pear wedges in a steamer basket and then lower the basket into the pot. Close the lid and turn clockwise to seal. 2. Press "MANUAL" and set the cooking time to 2 minutes. Cook on HIGH. When the timer goes off, move the pressure handle to "Venting" for a quick pressure release. 3. Open the lid carefully and take out the basket. Discard the water and wipe the Instant Pot clean. Press "SAUTE" and add in the coconut oil. 4. When melted, add the pears and cook until browned. Top with butter and serve.

Per Serving: Calories 395; Fat 37g; Sodium 105mg; Carbs 13g; Fiber 3g; Sugar 1g; Protein 10g

Aromatic Lemony Apples

Prep time: 10 minutes | Cook time: 3 minutes | Serves: 2

2 apples, peeled and cut into wedges
½ cup lemon juice
½ teaspoon cinnamon
1 tablespoon almond butter
1 cup water

1. Add and mix the lemon juice and water in the Instant Pot. 2. Place the apple wedges inside the steaming basket and lower the basket into the Instant Pot. Close the lid and turn clockwise to seal. 3. Select the "MANUAL" cooking mode. Set the cooking time to 3 minutes. Cook on HIGH pressure. When the timer goes off, press the "KEEP WARM/CANCEL" button. Turn the pressure handle from "Sealing" to "Venting" to release the pressure quickly. 4. Open the lid and remove the steaming basket. Place the apple wedges to a bowl. Drizzle with almond butter and sprinkle with cinnamon. 5. Serve and enjoy!

Per Serving: Calories 217; Fat 18g; Sodium 71mg; Carbs 19g; Fiber 8g; Sugar 0g; Protein 8g

Chocolate Almond Banana Squares

Prep time: 10 minutes | Cook time: 15 minutes | Serves: 6

½ cup almond butter

3 bananas

2 tablespoons cocoa powder

1½ cups water

1. Place the bananas and almond butter in a bowl and mash them finely with a fork. Add the cocoa powder and stir until well combined. 2. Grab a baking dish that can fit into the Instant Pot and grease it with some cooking spray. 3. Pour the banana and almond batter into the dish. Pour the water into the Instant Pot and lower the trivet. 4. Place the baking dish on top of the trivet and put the lid of the Instant Pot on. 5. Seal and then select the "MANUAL" cooking mode. Set the cooking time to 15 minutes. Cook on HIGH pressure. When the timer goes off, press the "KEEP WARM/CANCEL" button. Turn the handle to "Venting" and release the pressure quickly. 6. Open the lid and take out the baking dish. Let cool for a few minutes before cutting into squares. 7. Serve and enjoy!

Per Serving: Calories 260; Fat 21g; Sodium 71mg; Carbs 21g; Fiber 10g; Sugar 1g; Protein 11g

Tropical Coconut and Pear Delight

Prep time: 10 minutes | Cook time: 5 minutes | Serves: 2

¼ cup almond flour

1 cup coconut milk

2 large pears, peeled and diced

¼ cup shredded coconut, unsweetened

1. Mix all of the ingredients in the Instant Pot. Close the lid and turn clockwise to seal. Select "MANUAL" and set the cooking time to 5 minutes. Cook on HIGH pressure. 2. After the beep, press the "KEEP WARM/CANCEL" button. Turn the pressure handle to "Venting" so you can allow a quick pressure release. 3. Open the lid very carefully, keeping hands away from the steam. Divide the mixture between two bowls. Sprinkle with some cinnamon, if desired. Enjoy!

Per Serving: Calories 129; Fat 12g; Sodium 75mg; Carbs 9g; Fiber 1g; Sugar 1g; Protein 3g

Currant Poached Peaches

Prep time: 10 minutes | Cook time: 5 minutes | Serves: 4

½ cup black currants

4 peaches, peeled, pits removed

1 cup freshly squeezed orange juice

1 cinnamon stick

1. Place the black currants and the orange juice in a blender. Blend until the mixture becomes smooth. Pour the orange/currant mixture into the Instant Pot. 2. Add the cinnamon stick inside. Place the peaches inside the steamer basket. Lower the basket into the pot. 3. Close the lid and turn clockwise to seal. Select the "MANUAL" mode. Set the cooking time to 5 minutes. Cook on HIGH pressure. Press the "KEEP WARM/CANCEL" button after you hear the beep. 4. Turn the pressure handle to "Venting" for a quick pressure release and open the lid carefully. 5. Serve the peaches drizzled with the sauce. Enjoy!

Per Serving: Calories 136; Fat 13g; Sodium 11mg; Carbs 11g; Fiber 5g; Sugar 0g; Protein 2g

Delicious Apple and Peach Compote

Prep time: 10 minutes | Cook time: 8 minutes | Serves: 4

2½ cups peach pieces

2 cups diced apples

juice of 1 orange

2 tablespoon arrowroot

½ cup water

¼ teaspoon cinnamon

1. Place the peaches, apples, water, and orange juice, inside the Instant Pot. Stir to mix well and close the lid. Turn the lid clockwise to seal properly. 2. Select the "MANUAL" cooking mode and set the cooking time to 3 minutes. Cook on HIGH pressure. Select "KEEP WARM/CANCEL" after the beep. Turn the pressure handle to "Venting" for a quick pressure release and open the lid carefully. 3. Press the "SAUTE" button and Mix in the arrowroot. Cook until the compote is thickened, about 5 minutes or so. 4. Place the compote to an airtight container. Refrigerate for about 2 hours. Serve and enjoy!

Per Serving: Calories 367; Fat 31g; Sodium 285mg; Carbs 29g; Fiber 6g; Sugar 2g; Protein 14g

Cinnamon Strawberry Cream

Prep time: 10 minutes | Cook time: 3 hours | Serves: 15

2 tablespoons lemon juice
2 pounds strawberries, chopped
½ cup stevia
1 teaspoon cinnamon powder
1 teaspoon vanilla extract

1. In slow cooker, mix strawberries with stevia, lemon juice, cinnamon and vanilla, cover and cook on Low temp setting for 3 hours. 2. Blend a bit using an immersion blender, divide between bowls and keep In the fridge until you serve it. 3. Enjoy!

Per Serving: Calories 223; Fat 19g; Sodium 222mg; Carbs 13g; Fiber 2g; Sugar 1g; Protein 11g

Traditional Berry Pie

Prep time: 10 minutes | Cook time: 2 hours | Serves: 6

1 pound fresh blackberries
1 pound fresh blueberries
¾ cup water
5 tablespoons stevia
1 cup almond flour
½ cup arrowroot powder
1 teaspoon baking powder
⅓ cup coconut milk
1 egg, whisked
1 teaspoon lemon zest, grated
3 tablespoons coconut oil, melted

1. In slow cooker, mix blueberries, blackberries, stevia, water and half of the almond flour, cover and cook on High for 1 hour. 2. Meanwhile, in a bowl, mix the rest of the flour with arrowroot, and baking powder and stir well. 3. Add egg, milk, oil and lemon zest, stir, drop spoonfuls of this mix over the berries from the Crockpot, cover and cook on High for 1 more hour. 4. Leave pie aside to cool down, divide into dessert bowls and serve.

Per Serving: Calories 235; Fat 21g; Sodium 104mg; Carbs 21g; Fiber 2g; Sugar 1g; Protein 6g

Figs & Pecans Stuffed Apples

Prep time: 10 minutes | Cook time: 2 hours | Serves: 4

4 apples, tops cut off and cored
4 figs
2 tablespoons stevia
1 teaspoon ginger powder
¼ cup pecans, chopped
2 teaspoons lemon zest, grated
¼ teaspoon nutmeg, ground
½ teaspoon cinnamon powder
1 tablespoon lemon juice
1 tablespoon coconut oil
½ cup water

1. In a bowl, mix figs with stevia, ginger, pecans, lemon zest, nutmeg, cinnamon, oil and lemon juice, mix really well and stuff apples with this mix. 2. Put the water in slow cooker, Place apples, cover, cook on High for 2 hours, divide on dessert plates and serve. 3. Enjoy!

Per Serving: Calories 175; Fat 16g; Sodium 23mg; Carbs 12g; Fiber 2g; Sugar 1g; Protein 5g

Dark Chocolate Cake

Prep time: 10 minutes | Cook time: 3 hours | Serves: 10

1 cup almond flour
½ cup cocoa powder
3 tablespoons swerve
1 and ½ teaspoons baking powder
3 eggs
Cooking spray
4 tablespoons coconut oil, melted
¾ teaspoon vanilla extract
⅔ cup almond milk
⅓ cup keto chocolate chips

1. In a bowl, mix swerve with almond flour, cocoa powder, baking powder, milk, oil, eggs, chocolate chips and vanilla extract, mix really well, pour this into your lined and greased Crockpot and cook on Low temp setting for 3 hours. 2. Leave the cake aside to cool down, slice and serve.

Per Serving: Calories 139; Fat 13g; Sodium 112mg; Carbs 15g; Fiber 2g; Sugar 1g; Protein 3g

Lemon and berries Cream

Prep time: 30 minutes | Cook time: 1 hour | Serves: 4

1 cup coconut milk
Zest of 1 lemon, grated
6 egg yolks
1 cup coconut cream

1 cup water
3 tablespoons stevia
½ cup fresh blackberries

1. In slow cooker, mix coconut milk with lemon zest, mixed egg yolks, cream, water, stevia and blackberries, toss, cover and cook on High for 1 hour. 2. Divide between bowls and serve cold.

Per Serving: Calories 133; Fat 12g; Sodium 42mg; Carbs 12g; Fiber 2g; Sugar 1g; Protein 4g

Nutty Carrot Cake

Prep time: 10 minutes | Cook time: 4 hours | Serves: 4

5 ounces almond flour
¾ teaspoon baking powder
½ teaspoon baking soda
½ teaspoon cinnamon powder
¼ teaspoon nutmeg, ground
½ teaspoon allspice
1 egg
3 tablespoons coconut cream

2 tablespoons stevia
¼ cup water
4 tablespoons coconut oil, melted
½ cup carrots, grated
⅓ cup pecans, toasted and chopped
⅓ cup coconut flakes
Cooking spray

1. In a bowl, mix flour with baking soda and powder, allspice, cinnamon and nutmeg and stir. 2. In a second bowl, mix the egg with coconut cream, stevia, water, oil, carrots, pecans and coconut flakes and stir well. 3. Add and mix the two mixtures, stir very well everything, pour this into slow cooker slow cooker after you've greased it with cooking spray, cover and cook on low temp setting for 4 hours. 4. Leave the cake to cool down, then cut and serve it.

Per Serving: Calories 211; Fat 16g; Sodium 67mg; Carbs 13g; Fiber 4g; Sugar 5g; Protein 5g

Berries Cream

Prep time: 10 minutes | Cook time: 2 minutes | Serves: 2

⅓ cup blueberries
⅓ cup chopped strawberries
⅓ cup raspberries
1 cup coconut milk
¼ teaspoon vanilla extract

1. Place all of the ingredients, except the vanilla extract, inside the Instant Pot. Close the lid and seal. 2. Select the "MANUAL" cooking mode and set the cooking time to 2 minutes. Make sure to cook on HIGH pressure. When the timer goes off, press "KEEP WARM/CANCEL". 3. Turn the pressure handle to "Venting" for a quick pressure release and open the lid carefully. 4. Place the mixture to a blender. Add the vanilla extract and pulse until smooth. Divide between two serving glasses and place in the fridge. Refrigerate for 4 hours before serving. Enjoy!

Per Serving: Calories 173; Fat 13g; Sodium 394mg; Carbs 9g; Fiber 0g; Sugar 0g; Protein 12g

Energy Booster Bars

Prep time: 30 minutes | Cook time: 0 minutes | Serves: 6

¼ cup cocoa nibs
1 cup almonds, soaked for at least 3 hours
2 tablespoons cocoa powder
¼ cup hemp seeds
¼ cup goji berries
¼ cup coconut, shredded
8 dates, pitted and soaked

1. Put almonds in a food processor and blend them well. Add hemp seeds, cocoa nibs, cocoa powder, goji, coconut and blend well. Add dates gradually and blend some more. 2. Place mix to a parchment paper, spread and press it. Cut in equal pieces and serve after you've kept them in the fridge for 30 minutes. Enjoy!

Per Serving: Calories 181; Fat 15g; Sodium 36mg; Carbs 10g; Fiber 4g; Sugar 1g; Protein 6g

Stewed Figs and Pine Nuts

Prep time: 10 minutes | Cook time: 1 hour 20 minutes | Serves: 15

1 cup water
1 pound figs
½ cup pine nuts, toasted
4 tablespoons stevia

1. In slow cooker, mix figs with water, stevia and pine nuts, toss, cover and cook on High for 1 hour and 20 minutes. 2. Divide stewed figs into small bowls and serve them cold.

Per Serving: Calories 167; Fat 13g; Sodium 2mg; Carbs 22g; Fiber 4g; Sugar 2g; Protein 2g

Silky Strawberry Marmalade

Prep time: 10 minutes | Cook time: 3 hours | Serves: 6

4 and ½ cups strawberries
1 cup stevia
2 tablespoons ginger, grated
½ cup water

1. In slow cooker, mix strawberries with stevia, ginger and water, stir, cover and cook on High for 3 hours. 2. Divide marmalade into jars and serve as a dessert. Enjoy!

Per Serving: Calories 184; Fat 16g; Sodium 72mg; Carbs 9g; Fiber 2g; Sugar 1g; Protein 5g

Simple Raspberry Cream

Prep time: 10 minutes | Cook time: 2 hours | Serves: 4

3 tablespoons stevia
12 ounces raspberries
2 egg yolks, Mixed
2 tablespoons lemon juice
2 tablespoons coconut oil, melted

1. In slow cooker, mix raspberries with stevia, egg yolks, lemon juice and melted coconut oil, cover and cook on High for 2 hours. 2. Mix cream one more time, divide into small cups and serve cold. Enjoy!

Per Serving: Calories 136; Fat 12g; Sodium 33mg; Carbs 8g; Fiber 2g; Sugar 1g; Protein 2g

Almond Pomegranate Fudge

Prep time: 2 hours | Cook time: 5 minutes | Serves: 6

½ cup coconut milk
1 teaspoon vanilla extract
¼ cups cocoa butter
¾ cocoa powder
½ cup almonds, chopped
½ cup pomegranate seeds

1. Put milk in a pan and heat up over low heat. Add cocoa butter, cocoa powder and stir for 5 minutes. 2. Take off heat, add vanilla extract, half of the pomegranate seeds and half the of the nuts and stir. 3. Pour this into a lined baking pan, spread, sprinkle a pinch of salt, the rest of the pomegranate arils and nuts, cover and keep in the fridge for a few hours. 4. Cut, place on a platter and serve. Enjoy!

Per Serving: Calories 282; Fat 23g; Sodium 242mg; Carbs 13g; Fiber 1g; Sugar 2g; Protein 9g

Cashew Apple Stew

Prep time: 10 minutes | Cook time: 4 hours | Serves: 6

6 apples, cored, peeled and sliced
1 and ½ cups almond flour
Cooking spray
3 tablespoons stevia
1 tablespoon cinnamon powder
¾ cup cashew butter, melted

1. Grease slow cooker slow cooker with cooking spray, add apples, flour, stevia, cinnamon and cashew butter, stir gently, cover, cook on High for 4 hours, divide between bowls and serve cold. 2. Enjoy!

Per Serving: Calories 190; Fat 14g; Sodium 244mg; Carbs 10g; Fiber 1g; Sugar 1g; Protein 10g

Nuts and Berries Jelly

Prep time: 10 minutes | Cook time: 0 minutes | Serves: 2

1 pounds grapefruit jelly
½ pound coconut cream
A handful fresh berries for serving
A handful nuts, roughly chopped for serving

1. In a food processor, Add and mix grapefruit jelly with coconut cream and blend well. 2. Add berries and nuts, toss gently, Place to dessert cups and serve right away! 3. Enjoy!

Per Serving: Calories 151; Fat 14g; Sodium 64mg; Carbs 13g; Fiber 3g; Sugar 1g; Protein 2g

Conclusion

After completing the 30-Day Whole Foods Challenge, it's time to reflect on the experience. What was the most challenging part of the challenge? What did you learn about yourself? What are your thoughts on 30-Day Whole Foods now? The most challenging part of the challenge for me was giving up processed foods. I'm so used to eating packaged snacks and meals that it was hard to let go of that convenience. I also had to get used to cooking more meals from scratch. I learned that I enjoy cooking and eating whole foods. I feel so much better when I'm eating healthy, homemade meals. I also realized that I don't need processed foods to be happy or satisfied. Overall, I'm really happy that I completed the challenge. I feel better physically and mentally, and I'm proud of myself for committing to eating healthier. If you're considering doing the challenge of 30-Day Whole Foods, I say go for it! It's worth it.

Appendix 1 Measurement Conversion Chart

VOLUME EQUIVALENTS (LIQUID)

US STANDARD	US STANDARD (OUNCES)	METRIC (APPROXIMATE)
2 tablespoons	1 fl.oz	30 mL
¼ cup	2 fl.oz	60 mL
½ cup	4 fl.oz	120 mL
1 cup	8 fl.oz	240 mL
1½ cup	12 fl.oz	355 mL
2 cups or 1 pint	16 fl.oz	475 mL
4 cups or 1 quart	32 fl.oz	1 L
1 gallon	128 fl.oz	4 L

VOLUME EQUIVALENTS (DRY)

US STANDARD	METRIC (APPROXIMATE)
⅛ teaspoon	0.5 mL
¼ teaspoon	1 mL
½ teaspoon	2 mL
¾ teaspoon	4 mL
1 teaspoon	5 mL
1 tablespoon	15 mL
¼ cup	59 mL
½ cup	118 mL
¾ cup	177 mL
1 cup	235 mL
2 cups	475 mL
3 cups	700 mL
4 cups	1 L

TEMPERATURES EQUIVALENTS

FAHRENHEIT(F)	CELSIUS(C) (APPROXIMATE)
225 °F	107 °C
250 °F	120 °C
275 °F	135 °C
300 °F	150 °C
325 °F	160 °C
350 °F	180 °C
375 °F	190 °C
400 °F	205 °C
425 °F	220 °C
450 °F	235 °C
475 °F	245 °C
500 °F	260 °C

WEIGHT EQUIVALENTS

US STANDARD	METRIC (APPROXINATE)
1 ounce	28 g
2 ounces	57 g
5 ounces	142 g
10 ounces	284 g
15 ounces	425 g
16 ounces (1 pound)	455 g
1.5 pounds	680 g
2 pounds	907 g

Appendix 2 Recipes Index

"Hummus" of Spinach and Carrot 77

A

Almond and Coconut Apple Dessert 88
Almond Crusted Zucchini Slices 82
Almond Pomegranate Fudge 97
Antioxidant Nuts Mix 74
Aromatic Cinnamon Pork Chops 51
Aromatic Dill Carrots 33
Aromatic Lemony Apples 89
Avocado with Scrambled Eggs 22

B

Baby Kale Salad with Bacon Egg 15
Bacon and Veggie Omelet Cupcakes 88
Bacon Chicken Skewers 83
Baked Brussels Sprouts 37
Baked Garlicky Snapper 67
Berries Cream 95

C

Cajun French Fries 77
Caprese Eggplant Roll Ups 79
Carrots and Tomatoes Salad 81
Cashew Apple Stew 97
Catfish and Veggie Gumbo 63
Cheese and Tomatoes Stuffed Turkey 44
Cheese Bell Pepper and Olives Frittata 16
Cheese Chicken Meatballs 41
Cheesy Bok Choi Quiche 19
Cheesy Cauliflower 20
Cheesy Garlic Cod 71
Cheesy Ranch Chicken with Bacon 43
Cheesy Sausage Dip 82
Cheesy Tomatoes with Basil Dressing 84
Cheesy Tuna Spread 63
Chicken Tagine with Pomegranates Seeds 49
Chicken with Mushrooms 46
Chocolate Almond Banana Squares 90
Chocolate Cereal 17
Cinnamon Strawberry Cream 92
Cinnamon Waffle 21
Coconut Pancake 19
Cod and Cherry Tomatoes Platter 72
Colorful Summer Vegetable Bake 27
Crispy Bacon Omelets 21
Crispy Pork Roast 52
Crispy Squash Fries 76
Currant Poached Peaches 91
Curried Chicken with Sweet Potatoes & Peas 43

D

Dark Chocolate Cake 93
Delicious Apple and Peach Compote 91
Delicious Caprese Chicken 42
Delicious Chili Hash Browns 78
Delicious Citrusy Beef 57
Delicious Garlic Shrimp 66
Delicious Pear and Goose 42
Delicious Shrimp Sushi Rolls 69
Delicious Tomatoes & Cashews Casserole 16
Delicious Zucchini & Chicken Quiche 24

E

Easy Grilled Asparagus 27
Easy Pear Wedges 89
Egg and Beef Burgers 15
Eggs and Brussels Sprouts 22
Eggs Benedict 25
Energy Booster Bars 95

F

Figs & Pecans Stuffed Apples 93

G

Garlic Butter Lobster Tails 71
Garlicky Bell Pepper and Tomato 80
Garlicky Roast Lamb Leg 56
Grilled Chicken with Refreshing Cucumber Radish Salsa 39
Grilled Garlicky Oysters 70
Grilled herbed Chicken 40
Grilled Salmon with Avocado Salsa 68
Grilled Shrimp Skewers 64
Grilled T-Bone Steaks 59

H

Healthy Cabbage Slaw 36
Healthy Cabbage, Carrot & Apple Stew 35
Healthy Chicken Zucchini Cutlets 46
Healthy Pumpkin Sandwich 18
Healthy Tuna Steaks with Noodles 69
Herbed Button Mushrooms 80
Herbed Eggplant Slices 29
Herbed Garlicky Wings 45
Herbed Spaghetti Squash 35
Homemade Carrot & Pecan Muffins 20
Hot Barbequed Steak 53

I

Italian-Style Turkey Breasts   39

J

Juicy Chicken with Blueberry Lime Salsa   48
Juicy Pork Chops   52

L

Lemon and berries Cream   94
Lemony Halibut   64
Lime Pork Tenderloin with Kale   59

M

Marinated Spiced Eggs   78
Mashed Coconut Pumpkin   28
Mexican-style Beef Stew   55
Mushroom Sliders   23

N

Nuts and Berries Jelly   98
Nutty Carrot Cake   94
Nutty Carrots   79

O

Onion Cucumber Salad   37

P

Pineapple Pork Roast   60
Pineapple Salad with Avocado   75
Pork in Wine Marinade   56
Pork Roast with Yucca   55
Prosciutto Wrapped Chicken Breasts   45
Pulled Pork with Barbeque Sauce   60

R

Refreshing Shrimp Salad   72
Roasted Potatoes   74

S

Salmon and Tomato Stew   65
Salmon Bake   62
Salmon Nori Rolls   65
Sausage and Mushroom Frittata   18
Savory Beans with Bacon   30
Savory Sweet Potatoes   85
Sea Bass with Juicy Broccoli   66
Silky Strawberry Marmalade   96
Simple Kale and Celery Dish   34
Simple Paprika Potato Slices   76
Simple Raspberry Cream   96
Smoky Baby Back Ribs   54
Sour Turkey Breasts   47
Spiced Broccoli   29
Spiced Chicken   40
Spiced Tofu and Zucchini Skewers   31
Spiced Turkey Wings   75
Spiced Whole Chicken   44
Spicy Barbecued Spareribs   51
Spicy Cajun Roast Beef   53
Spicy Lemony Swordfish   67
Squash and Sweet Potato Soup   33
Stewed Chicken with Veggies   47
Stewed Figs and Pine Nuts   96
Sweet Potato Sticks   81

T

Tangy Apple Pork Ribs   54
Tangy Pork Chops and Mushrooms   57
Tasty Goat Skewers   83
Tasty Tiger Prawns and Bitter Melon   62
Tasty Tuna Stuffed Tomatoes   31
Tender Baked Haddock   68
Teriyaki Pork Ribs   58
Thai Chicken and Veggie Stew   41
Tomato Gazpacho   36
Tomato Pasta with Basil   32
Tortilla Chips   86
Traditional Beef Ragu   58
Traditional Berry Pie   92
Traditional White Fish Curry   70
Tropical Coconut and Pear Delight   90
Turkey and Broccoli Balls   48

V

Vegetable Quiche   23
Vegetables Roast   34
Veggies and Egg Casserole   17

Y

Yummy Broccoli and Hazelnuts   32

Z

Zucchini Slaw   28
Zucchini with Scrambled Eggs   30

Made in the USA
Las Vegas, NV
12 April 2023

70509097R00062